Black Mountain Elegy

Other Books by Eddie Nickels

Marine Corps Draftee:

A Vietnam Era Draftee's Personal Experiences of Parris Island and Infantry Training Regiment

Six Years to Live:

An Odyssey of Life, Death, and Adversity

Garfield versus Marshall:

The Civil War Battles and Skirmishes in the Mountains of Southeastern Kentucky and Southwestern Virginia

Scotia: Coal Mine of Doom:

The Tragic Coal Mine Explosions of March 9 and 11, 1977

BLACK MOUNTAIN ELEGY

THE REMINISCES of a SCOTIA COAL MINER

EDDIE NICKELS

Black Mountain Elegy: The Reminisces of a Scotia Coal Miner

ISBN 978-0-9886933-5-7

In memory of the forty one coal miners who lost their lives inside Scotia's Big Black Mountain operations between May, 1962, through December, 1991.

Contents

Acknowledgements

There's more to writing a book than just jotting down some remembrances and typing the words on a sheet of paper. Without the help of friends and family, by providing photos, suggestions, moral support and last but not least, helpful critique, putting together a book would be an overwhelming experience, to say the least.

My former Scotia co-worker, Mike Halcomb, provided many photos and documents included in this book and offered to help in any way he could. His photos and information on the Scotia Rescue teams was a wonderful addition to the book, and I will always be grateful for his help and cooperation.

Mike is not just a former co-worker but one of my best friends during my time at Scotia. I want to acknowledge and thank Mike for allowing me to use the photo of a quilt that was pieced together using parts of Scotia Mine Rescue clothing. This could easily be an item of possible historical significance concerning the now defunct coal mining company.

I can't say enough about the excellent technical support given me by my grandson, Joshua Dylan Nickels. I don't believe this book would have been possible without his knowledge and computer savvy. His photography skills, formatting knowledge, and attention to detail were extremely helpful to me. I owe him a debt of gratitude for all the time he devoted to help with the editing and formatting of the book. A big time publisher has nothing on him for sure. He is a master of the keyboard and his writing and analytical skills were invaluable to me in the production of this book.

Thanks also to friends who encourage me from time to time continue with my writing endeavors. The enjoyment of reading and writing is a big factor in my life and I am grateful to God and country for the freedom to be able to express myself without fear of retribution or censorship.

Introduction

In 1962, the Blue Diamond Coal Company of Knoxville, Tennessee, acquired a large boundary of coal reserves which were located in and around the sparsely settled community of Oven Fork, Kentucky. This little community was located in Letcher County, Kentucky, and was about 14 miles in distance from Cumberland, Kentucky, In Harlan County, and about 16 miles from Whitesburg, Kentucky, in Letcher County.

In the beginning of mining operations, the Imboden seam of coal was to be mined, where the coal seam averaged six to seven feet in height under Big Black Mountain, and was considered to be a high quality coal for use in steel mills and in power plants to generate electricity. The Imboden seam of coal was below the water table and was considered a "gassy" mine because of the high concentrations of methane liberated over an average 24 hour period. According to the Mining Enforcement and Safety Administration (MESA) the Scotia mine liberated an average of 200,000 to 500,000 cubic feet of methane every 24 hours and was considered by MESA as the "most gassy" mine in Eastern Kentucky.

BLACK MOUNTAIN ELEGY

Because of the excessive amount of methane gas liberated in the Imboden seam, the ventilation of the mine presented difficulties in keeping the methane concentrations swept from all areas of the mine. This would result in tragic consequences on March 9 and 11, 1976, when two tragic explosions caused the deaths of 26 men, including 23 Scotia miners and three Federal Mine Inspectors. The eleven victims of the second explosion would be sealed in the mine for over eight months before their bodies were recovered.

In the years following the explosions, Scotia Coal Company would continue their coal producing operations, including producing coal in three new mine openings in the 1970's which were located above the original #1 Scotia mine. The Upper Taggart, New Taggart, and B Seam mines, which were well above the water table and therefore had few methane gas problems. They were located higher up the side of Black Mountain and in lower seams of coal. The company continued producing high quality coal for marketing in the late 1970's and in the 1980's, but a downturn in the market for coal in the late 1980's and early 1990's resulted in the selling of their Scotia operations by the parent company, Blue Diamond Coal Company, in 1990 to the Arch Mineral Corporation of St. Louis Missouri.

A name change to the Cumberland River Coal Company and the investment of $13 million dollars did not result in improved production numbers or improved cost efficiency and the Scotia Coal Company eventually ceased operations at Oven Fork and lay off their workforce.

This book is the personal experiences of one of those Scotia miners who worked inside Scotia's Black Mountain operations for over 17 years and who helped recover the bodies of the eleven men who were victims of the second explosion, then helped recover and re-ventilate the #1 mine for the production of coal. For those of us who worked there, those tragic days with their sad memories of Big Black Mountain will never fade.

While those memories are full of sadness for the loss of over 41 men in the Scotia mine over the mine's nearly 30 years of existence, we will at the same time always remember with fondness the people we met and worked with. They each have their own stories of life and death, and their own legacies will forever survive the closing of the Scotia mine and its storied history of being the "gassiest mine in Eastern Kentucky."

CHAPTER ONE

As Jimmy's Volkswagen "Bug" was chugging up the hill towards the Upper Taggart coal seam that September morning in 1974, I felt apprehensive about facing my first day as a coal miner. My stomach was tied in knots and my heart was pounding with the prospect of going underground for the first time since my dad had allowed me to go underground with him for a few hours when I was eight years old. That day ended in a bad experience for me when I pinched my finger between the welded steel of the old rail car we rode inside the mine. I was lucky I hadn't lost a finger that day. The experience taught me that coal mining was a dangerous proposition for eight year old boys and twenty seven year old men facing their first day as a coal miner.

My younger brother Jimmy had picked me up at the Scotia Coal Company's parking area located at the foot of the hill that Scotia's Upper Taggart underground mine was located in. He was a cutting machine operator on the same section that I had been assigned to and offered me a ride to familiarize me with the road to the mine.

BLACK MOUNTAIN ELEGY

As we pulled into the parking lot adjacent to the Old Taggart mine office I stared at the four mine openings that were equally spaced along the ridge line of the mountain hillside. I was shocked and dismayed as I stared at the openings. How on earth do they get men and equipment inside those tiny openings, I wondered? I had been warned that the section I had been assigned to was very low and that my height and girth would make my introduction to mining difficult and intimidating until I could get accustomed to the rigors involved in "digging coal". As I stared at the hillside I was in total agreement with their admonition of difficulty of adjusting from the ease of carrying an order book and writing pen to mining coal for a living.

The transformation from a traveling salesman for a wholesale grocery company to a prospective coal miner had its roots in the color green, as in the color of money. (At least it used to be green.)

Jimmy had worked for the same grocery company I worked for and had left for a job with Scotia because of the better pay involved. We were talking about his new job when we were visiting our parent's home and he casually pulled out his pay stub for that week and showed me why he changed jobs. His pay for a week was almost exactly my pay for two weeks. I was hooked after that and he offered to speak with an acquaintance of his who worked in Scotia's mine office to see if I might possibly be able to get a job there also.

I decided to "test the waters" with Scotia and around the middle of August I took my scheduled vacation days and dropped by Scotia's mine office at their tipple site and put my application in. I knew from Jimmy that they were then hiring inexperienced miners but still one needed a little "pull" to get on there. I really had no expectation as to being hired immediately, even if I eventually managed to get an interview.

As I finished the application and handed it to the secretary in the mine office I turned and headed out the door to my vehicle parked in the parking area. I had only walked a few feet when I heard someone shout my name. As I turned around I saw the secretary waving me back to the office.

Thinking that I might have missed an item or two on the application I walked back into the office and she said, "We've been waiting for you, Jimmy has already told us about you!" With those words I wondered just what he might have told them about me to get me on there without any mining experience!

The company where I was then employed had been very good to work for and I dreaded to tell them I was leaving for another job but they were very understanding and wished me the best in the new job. They also offered me a little more salary if I decided to change my mind.

While taking my earned vacation days I shopped for a mining hat and a mining belt to carry the paraphernalia a miner must have on his belt in order to survive underground. At the time of my hiring, a mining light, (supplied by the company), a MSA Self-Rescuer, (a canister that affords temporary protection from the effects of carbon monoxide and/or smoke), and a name or number tag was issued to be carried on each individual's leather or nylon mining belt.

The mining hat was of a hard plastic material and had to be painted yellow for a new miner of less than one year's experience in or around a mine. The hat I managed to find and purchase resembled a World War One French soldier's helmet more than the hat that most Scotia miners then wore. The yellow paint made it look even more outlandish. I got rid of it and obtained a more appropriate white painted mining hat after my first year as a miner.

My wife, Wanda, and my young children, Steven, age seven, Alisha, age five, and Jeffrey, age two, were also apprehensive of my changing jobs as even they were aware of the dangers pertaining to the coal industry. After all, they had heard stories and discussions between me and other relatives about my own maternal grandfather G.C. Sexton's premature death when working as a brakeman inside a Thornton, Kentucky coal drift mine in December, 1940.

My dad and mom were also skittish about having two of their sons working in a mine that already had a somewhat notorious reputation for having "bad top" and for being a "gassy" mine.[1] It was common knowledge among miners that Scotia was considered the most "gassy" mine in the whole state of Kentucky. Despite their and my own reservations about Scotia I made my plans and was determined to see them through, even though I might have to "eat crow" if the change I was making turned out to be a boondoggle of a decision.

One thing in particular worried my dad about us working in a non-UMW mine was that when the United Mine Workers went on strike occasionally while negotiating a new contract the Scotia mine might be subjected to picketing and possible violence of some sort or other?

His concern was based on the fact that just recently, (January 1967), Scotia had been picketed by striking

---

[1] Scotia's # 1 mine liberated in the range of 200,000 to 500.000 cubic feet of methane per 24 hour period.

miners of Local Union 1435, United Mine Workers of America.

"Please do not cross our picket line," the members of Local Union 1435, United Mine Workers of America, ask in an advertisement concerning their strike against Scotia Coal Company at Oven Fork, which began June 1. ("We) urgently request that no coal miner seek employment with this company," Lloyd Long, president of the Local Union says in the ad.

The UMWA had opened an organizing drive at Scotia in September, 1965 even though the Southern Labor Union was still the Scotia employees bargaining agent at that time. Scotia workers voted in favor of UMWA representation but talks having broken down by June, 1966, the Scotia miners came out on strike. Blue Diamond Mining, (the owners of Scotia) then hired strikebreakers to work the mine and on July 15, 1966, 42 Scotia miners crossed the picket line and went back to work. The UMWA stopped trying to organizing the Scotia miners after that. In 1967 Scotia employees formed their own union, the Scotia Employees Union, which was certified by the NLRB (National Labor Relations Board.)

A lasting reminder of Scotia's labor troubles was an old black van that sat beside the road near the entrance into the mining complex for many years. Many bullet holes were prominently evident in the body of the old van with many of us that passed there every day wondering what the mysterious history of that old vehicle might project if it could only talk to us.

The night before my first scheduled workday I slept very little because I felt a little trepidation as to whether or not I was making the right decision for my family.

The next day, September 2, 1974, was my first scheduled workday on the 2nd or evening shift at Scotia. I left for work at 12 Noon, even though the evening shift started work at 2:00 p.m. each day. I wanted to make sure I was on time.

I crossed over Pine Mountain (a mountain range of the Cumberland Mountains) and down into the Cumberland River water shed to Oven Fork and the Scotia entrance. I noticed that the guard stationed at the guard shack located about 400 yards from the main road (highway 119), was the same man that I had met at a Hazard medical facility when he and I took our physical for employment at Scotia.

He motioned me on through and I proceeded to park my '69 Chevy station wagon in the lower parking lot above the Scotia complex. I walked to the bath house below the parking area and waited for a while until Jimmy came in and picked me up to show me the route to our work place.

I had been given a choice of working in the #1 Scotia mine located behind the mine office or working in the Upper Taggart mine where my brother worked. I chose Upper Taggart which might have been a decision that could have likely saved my life nearly two years later when tragedy would strike Scotia Coal Company and Blue Diamond Coal Company of Knoxville, Tennessee, the owner of Scotia Coal Company. If I had known that the bottom (#1 mine) would experience two explosions and that 26 men would die in those tragic disasters I would never have been a coal miner and would have just turned around and went back home.

CHAPTER TWO

As Jimmy and I crawled out of his Volkswagen he approached me and handed me a face mask, saying, "Eddie I picked up an extra dust mask from the supply house, you'll need this when you get inside." I looked the mask over and saw that it had a rubber gasket in front and a flapper like gasket on each side of the mask with two elastic ties to tie the mask around the wearer's head.

It was the first time for me to see such a contraption and had quite a time getting it arranged just right around my noggin. I didn't know it at the time but both Jimmy and I would come to rely on those flimsy masks to keep gobs of coal dust and rock dust out of our nostrils and mouths. There was just one problem with that though; it seems that in later years a determination was made by the experts that the masks did little or no good. We suspected it at the time and those of us who wore them constantly took a lot of ribbing about it, but they were all we had and we weren't aware at the time that they were nearly, if not totally, worthless.

Regardless, and in spite of the coal and rock dust that permeated around the supposedly airtight seals, my brother and I were seldom without our dust mask on while we were inside. It seems the scoffers were right in their ribbing and fun-making of those of us who relied on them for protection.

Walking into the Upper Taggart mine office I introduced myself to the mine foreman and shook his hand. He asked about my mining experience and when I told him I had no experience he grinned and said, "You'll do fine, just look where you're walking when you're inside." If he had been honest with me he would've said instead, "Watch where you're crawling when you're inside!"

He assigned me to my brother's section where the boss was Sonny Cornett. He introduced me to Sonny who told me to stand by and just follow his crew as they loaded into the mantrip, the first time I had ever heard that word.

He directed me to the adjoining room, the lighthouse, where there were rough wooden benches around the room on which the miners were sitting and "shooting the breeze." They knew I was a newly hired inexperienced miner because of my yellow painted hat and probably by my nervousness. I tried to buckle my headlamp battery onto my very new leather mining belt with an equally shiny self-rescuer and brass man number shining on my belt. Somehow I managed to put it on correctly while the men were speculating as to whether I would emerge from the mine alive at the end of the shift. I was expecting some little harassment on this, my first day and I wasn't disappointed.

I noticed that the men (numbering fifty or so) were dressed for work in the attire that suited one's taste and varied greatly among them. Some wore long sleeve shirts, some short sleeved, some had on coats or jackets, some none. Many were wearing rubber boots, indicating that they were either expecting to work or wade in water or in case they might work around electrical equipment. Some, like me, had on leather boots which were more comfortable to walk (crawl) in. I noticed that most miners had plastic tape tightly wrapped around their trousers at the top of their pants and their sleeve cuffs were also taped. This was done as a safety measure to help prevent loose clothing from possibly getting caught in the machinery and equipment used in the mine. As experienced miners they dressed for labor, not for comfort. Like the soldiers of the Confederacy of 110 years before, they were dressed mostly as it pleased themselves.

As we headed outside to load into the mantrips I noted that a low locomotive powered by a four foot long wooden arm that had a metal hook on the end that was attached to a large naked copper wire hung on hangers leading into the mine. This appeared at first glance to be a highly dangerous apparatus (which it was) and I wondered who the genius was that came up with this idea. As time passed I learned that the system was a practical one and was as safe as anything else was when underground.

A word here about the mantrip cars themselves: they were simply made, consisting of welded metal about 32 inches in height and with barely enough room to slide in sideways, four men to a compartment. Of course if one or two of the men happened to be on the hefty side, three would fill up a compartment. There were three compartments in each car of the mantrip, and usually two or three metal cars hooked to each locomotive, one car for each section of the mine.

The railcar we were assigned was coupled next to the low vain locomotive and I ended up on the outside edge of the car. I squeezed myself into the small opening with difficulty, and wondered how in the world the large man beside me managed to successfully negotiate through the small opening that served as a doorway into the low car. When I say low, I mean low, as our noses barely cleared the top of the vehicle.

As the locomotive started into the mine we went through a line "curtain" stretched across the track so as to keep the fresh air from short circuiting when going into or coming out of the mine. As the cars rolled over the 60# rails [2] the rails clicked and clacked as the steel wheels traveled across the fishplates.[3]

The timbers that were set along the track and in between the breaks were flying by, it seemed to me. I felt that we were going way too fast for the condition of the rails, but as the new man on the block who was I to complain about that of which I knew next to nothing about? In reality the locomotive wasn't traveling very fast at all, it's just the lying on one's side in low top in an enclosed vehicle gives the illusion of high speed even when that speed isn't very high at all.

After about a fifteen minute jolting ride we reached the end of the track on our particular section. (There were several sections scattered throughout the mine, at least three others besides the one I was assigned to.) As the locomotive rolled to a stop I rolled out of the mantrip car and got to my knees and moved out of the path of the other miners who rolled out of the cramped compartments and quickly started on their way into the ebony depths of the mine with every man's head lamp weaving and bobbing as they rushed towards the section where they would be producing coal.

---

[2] Every yard length of rail weighted 60#.
[3] Plates that joined two rails together

While waiting for others to take the lead I shined my lamp into the blackness and could see nothing but white ribs and long blocks of coal with openings (breaks) every 80 feet or so for men and equipment to be able to travel from place to place inside the mine and on the coal mining section. The blocks of coal were all of fairly equal size, 80' in length and 60'wide.

Everything was new and strange to me as a new miner and I had a lot to learn before I could understand everything I was seeing and hearing. It's a wonder that any new and inexperienced miner can avoid getting hurt or killed their first few days in an environment that is totally different than they have ever seen or been exposed to in the outside world.

After exiting the small compartment on the mantrip, I got to my knees and noticed that the mine roof was so low that walking could be accomplished by "duck walking" or by bending one's self completely over with the head nearly touching the knees. I knew immediately that I was in deep doo doo.

A feeling of complete helplessness washed over me as I thought, "How in the world am I going to be able to negotiate this low space to reach the section? I thought for a moment that I would jump back into that mantrip car and go back outside with the motorman, but my pride wouldn't let me. Actually the locomotive was already moving or maybe I would have jumped in with him and go to where a man could stand up and breathe fresh air.

The section foreman, (Sonny), crawled up beside me and told me to take my time getting to the working section and that the large man who was in the compartment with me on the mantrip would walk to the section with me. He turned to Bill and told him to show me the way to the section. I was thankful for the company as I realized if they left me on my own I was totally in the dark (no pun intended) as to where I was heading and how far the trip was to the working face.

As most of the crew took off and their lights faded into the blackness ahead, Bill and I started slowly following their trail with me bending over as far as I possibly could while walking. Bill was also having a tough time of it and would walk a few feet, then crawl a few feet. I was emulating him the best I could but I found myself doing more crawling and duck walking than bent over walking.

The height of the mine roof was between 40 and 45 inches, the varying height conforming to the contour of the slate roof. Since Bill and I were both over six foot tall we were both struggling to move even a few feet forward while having to stop to rest every few feet we managed to advance. At one point I managed to ask Bill how far it was to the working face area and he replied, "Well I reckon it's at least twenty breaks, if not more!"

My heart sank as I quickly did the math in my head and realized we had to travel around 1,600 feet before we even reached the section. I wondered to myself if we could make it before lunch time.

After a long period of time we eventually reached the section, with both Bill and me drenched in sweat and panting like wounded panthers. I was in no shape just then for any gainful activity and neither was Bill, but he, after a few minutes rest, left the "dinner hole" area to climb into his shuttle car's operating deck to begin his shift of work hauling coal from the working face to the beltline "feeder."

After I caught my breath and had a little rest Sonny took me to the beltline feeder and told me my job that night was to keep the coal shoveled from in front of the feeder so the shuttle cars could dump their coal into the feeder without getting stuck in the loose coal.

CHAPTER THREE

It didn't take much shoveling for me to feel as though my arms weighed a ton and for my arm muscles to feel as though they couldn't lift another shovelful, even though the shift had just started. Each time a shuttle car dumped a load they spilled so much loose coal over their sides that they were spilling more than I could shovel between loads. Eventually both car drivers had to spend a few minutes each time as they pulled up to the feeder to grab an extra shovel and help me shovel some of the spilled coal. Without their help it would have been a long night for me.

I hadn't been shoveling too long when I saw the face crew in the same entry I was in, about five breaks from where I was located. I didn't know what they were doing but I could see their lights on their equipment and hear the loud noise of that equipment running.

A few minutes later I heard someone shout, "FIRE, fire, fire!" Immediately afterward I saw the flash of a blinding light mixed with flame as a tremendous blast reverberated throughout the whole mine, it seemed. I threw my shovel down and my mining hat and light fell into the roadway as I fell to the mine floor.

As the coal dust was settling from the blast I tried to make sense of what had just happened. My mind was racing with the fact that here it was, my first day in the mine and it had blown up! I almost panicked when I realized that I didn't know where to go or what to do in that situation. Thankfully, after a few moments I saw a light on a shuttle car as it made its way to the feeder where I was still reeling from the explosion and my mind was still confused.

As the driver pulled up to the feeder I shouted, "What happened up there?" He had a slight grin as he explained that this was a conventional section which meant that the coal face had to be drilled and powder sticks had to be inserted into the holes to shoot the coal from the face of the coal seam. Somehow I had neglected to ask how the coal was mined at the face and just took for granted that all the coal was mined at Scotia using continuous mining machines to dig the coal out. I didn't bother telling the shuttle car driver that I had thought for a while that the section had blown up during my very first day as a miner! I had a lot to learn, it seems.

Helping me to shovel the loose coal was especially hard on my walking buddy who had walked from the end of the track to the section with me. He had a rough time just getting in and out of the deck of the shuttle car, much less having to help me shovel between loads. But somehow I, and we, persisted, and after what seemed like many hours of shoveling the black gold, I was told by one of the car drivers that it was dinnertime for them and me. I thought it would never come so I didn't argue with them when they called me to dinner, which always took place at the "dinner hole" where the 7,200 volt power center was located.

The men (and they were all men) congregated at the power center because the main power box was always very warm and made an ideal place to sit and stay warm while eating their dinner. Every section of men inside the mine did this routinely, even though it was against company rules and also against mining laws.

My dining choices for my first day in the mine turned out to totally detrimental to my having to stoop so low to get around in the low coal. I had packed my brand new black dinner bucket with a quart of orange juice to drink while working and the acidity of the juice made the rest of the shift miserable for me the rest of the shift. Even worse was the fact that I had also brought a medium chunk of raw cabbage for dinner. I can't begin to tell you how miserable I was after combining the cabbage and orange juice together. For a couple of hours I suffered terribly with a stomach ache and acid attack. I learned a painful but good lesson that there are some food items and liquids that just don't blend well with coal mining, especially in low coal.

At the end of the shift we walked or crawled to the end of the section track where the mantrip was already waiting for us. It took me and my companion of the earlier trek to the section working face much longer to reach the end of the track but they thankfully waited on us as we slowly and painfully made our way to the end of the section track. We did receive a few cat calls and choice words from the other members of our crew who had been waiting rather patiently for us to make our journey towards the waiting mantrip.

As we finally loaded up and proceeded towards the outside I once again watched as the timbers that were holding up the loose rock on the trackway seemed to fly by at a very fast clip. Several minutes later we reached the outside and we were finally able to breathe in the cool night air and I was able to get the kinks out of my poor aching back. After experiencing the confinement of the low roof and the tight spaces of the Upper Taggart section we had just left, I was more appreciative of being able to stand up straight than I had ever been in my life.

I also had a new and profound respect of the men and women who worked so hard in the coal mines of our country to (at that time) supply the fuel for most of our country's electricity needs. No wonder coal miners were earning such high wages at that time. I felt that I had earned the $46.46 I was being paid for my day's work beneath Black Mountain that day.

As we proceeded inside the lighthouse and put our cap lights on charge, Jimmy asked how I liked my first shift underground. I told him that I had an exciting time but not in a good way. I had seen him only once while on the section and that was at the dinner hole where I had mentioned to him and everyone else that I thought the whole mine had exploded at the time the first dynamite charge was set off in the face area. He had a good chuckle concerning that event and even I thought that it was mighty comical even if the joke was on me.

We climbed into his "Bug" and traveled on a very dusty dirt road back to the bathhouse located at the bottom of the mountain. The hot water of the showers felt so good after the coldness of the outside fall season. The water was hard water due to the high mineral and sulfur content but it was hot and wet and we managed to get most of the cold dust and rock dust washed off our tired bodies.

After showering I walked to the parking lot and slowly crawled under the steering wheel of my '69 Chevy and drove back across the curvy Pine Mountain highway towards Colson and home. I was so tired that I could barely manage to change gears in the standard shift as I crossed the mountain but the many gear changes helped me to stay awake at least.

When I arrived home Wanda was still up and waiting on me with a hot supper cooked. I wasn't in the mood for food so late at night but I managed to eat a little something before I had to try to get some sleep. I need not have worried about getting to sleep because after Wanda asked me how my day went I only managed to relate the highlights of my first day in the mine before sleep overcame me at last.

The next morning I woke up to soreness in my body and legs I had never experienced before. I could barely lift my legs to take a step. Jimmy had warned me that soreness would be a problem because of the low top and having to stoop over or crawl around while inside the mine. He advised me that it would take at least two weeks to work the soreness out of my arms and legs and he was certainly right about his prediction.

The soreness was by far the worst I had ever felt, even while training in the swamps of Parris Island during the Vietnam War era. I could barely raise my legs to go up the steps of my dad and mom's house because of the effort needed to step up each stair step.

Each day over the next two weeks was a trial for me while in the mine each night, not only because of the hard work but also because of working in the low top and still struggling each day to crawl to the section I was on. I questioned my decision to change jobs for such harsh working conditions, many times a day. It was only after I received my first paycheck after two weeks of work that I finally accepted my decision as being the right one when the higher rate of pay was considered.

After all, it's always about the money and the money was better at Scotia than anywhere else I had been employed. My family no longer had to struggle from payday to payday like we had been doing since our marriage in 1964. Even while I was in the military Wanda had to work to make ends meet. The $84.00 a month the military paid me in 1966 was the low point of my working life so far. At Scotia I was paid more than that for two days work and for work that was not much harder than the work I had to do while in the military.

While at Upper Taggart I was used mostly as a utility man, shoveling the feeder, shoveling the coal from the beltline each day and scattering rock dust on the sides, bottom, and top of a cut of coal after the scoop machine had done its job of scooping the loose coal from the working face.

Rock dusting was a necessary and important job of protecting a mine from explosions by scattering it on the coal dust and all mining entries. It was also a dirty job that required a dust mask to keep as many of the dust particles out of one's lungs as possible. My brother and I wore a dust mask practically all the time and despite our efforts some dust always seemed to be able to permeate the masks, which caused us to suffer some violent coughing spells after rock dusting an area.

They didn't seem to filter much dust, if any, but at least we had a feeling of a small amount of protection while wearing them. The coughing afterwards always seemed to result in some little amount of dust mixed with plenty of phlegm being expelled from the lungs, nose, and throat. Is it any wonder that so many coal miners end up with black lung and/or pneumoconiosis?

Although rock dusting can be hazardous to the health of a coal miner the Federal Government requires its application in all bituminous underground coal mines as stipulated in the announcement below in the Federal Register of June, 2011:

Mine operators are required to apply rock dust in underground bituminous coal mines to reduce the explosion potential of coal dust and other dust generated during mining operations. Effective and frequent rock dust application is essential to protect miners from the potential of a coal dust explosion, or if one occurs, to reduce its severity.

Where rock dust is required to be applied, it shall be distributed upon the top, floor, and sides of all underground areas of a coal mine and maintained in such quantities that the incombustible content of the combined coal dust, rock dust, and other dust shall be not less than 65 per centum, but the incombustible content in the return air courses shall be no less than 80 per centum. Federal Register/Vol. 76, No. 119/ June 21, 2011

One interesting incident from my short time at Upper Taggart is one involving the cap lamp. The cap lamp we used at the time of my employment at Scotia and for the whole time I worked there was the Koehler Wheat rechargeable battery-powered incandescent lamp.

This one item was one of the most important and handy items that we carried on our persons while underground. The Wheat light was invented by a miner named Grant Wheat in 1918 and was manufactured by the Koehler firm in Marlborough, Massachusetts. All coal miners own a debt of gratitude to Mr. Wheat for his invention which revolutionized miners cap lamps for the better. In the years before the Wheat lamp, miners had to depend on the mostly unreliable and somewhat cumbersome carbide lamp for use inside the mines of America and the world. My dad actually continued wearing his carbide lamp into the 1950's when he operated his own truck mine.

The Wheat lamp we used had a connecting 4 volt 6"x 8" battery that had a 4' cord attached to the head lamp which used a powerful incandescent bulb encased inside the lamp. The battery was a "wet" battery which usually required the addition of distilled water between shifts. This required the services of the "lighthouse man" who was responsible for keeping the Wheat batteries watered along with his other duties as the bathhouse attendee.

Usually one of the most senior men held this job although sometimes a slightly injured miner was offered temporary duty in the lighthouse and bath house in order to help him continue to draw his regular pay. This was considered a "pie" job but in fact carried much responsibility with it.

The incident involving the cap lamp I spoke of happened around my first couple of days underground. Every time I watched a shuttle car driver pull up to the feeder to dump a load of coal on the beltline I would shine my cap light directly into their eyes to see who and what they looked like and who they were. Like all new miners I thought your cap lamp should shine directly into someone's eyes when you were talking to them.

The first few times you do this the one who is the victim of such a bright light being shined directly into their eyes will only wince or turn their head from the bright light. Eventually they will tire of it and will chew out even a newbie that they have just met for the offence of nearly blinding them.

In my own greenhorn experience of blinding the shuttle car drivers, they took the blinding brightness for a trip or two then finally, as one of the drivers rounded the corner and I shined the full force of my powerful cap light into his eyes, he screamed out at me, "Get that mother f-----g light out of my eyes!" His shout was so loud I heard it even over the loud noise of the coal crushing roller that was part of the feeder. It was then that I realized that I had committed a no-no in mining and never forgot the lesson.

For years after this incident I too was the recipient of a light being shined directly into my eyes by a newly hired inexperienced miner from time to time, since Scotia always hired many people, both men and women, that had no or very little mining experience. I for one always appreciated the fact that the owners of Scotia, Blue Diamond Coal Company of Knoxville, Tennessee, would take a chance on nearly anyone willing to work hard and work safe.

CHAPTER FOUR

As I stepped into the light house on the evening of September 13th I was approached by our section boss Sonny who asked me if I'd like to get on a section that had higher coal and better working conditions and I quickly answered in the affirmative. I had heard that the new mine opening was a much better place to work in than the Upper Taggart section I had been assigned to.

Sonny then told me to report to the New Taggart mine Monday evening at 2:30 p.m. which suited me just fine since I was really struggling in the low top I had been working in. I didn't know whether he was trying to do me a favor or was trying to get rid of me but it made no difference. I was just glad to be looking forward to work in high top for a change.

New Taggart was located about a half-mile from Upper Taggart on a different ridge of Black Mountain and one had to take a different road up the mountain to reach the mining site. The road was newer and in better shape than the one leading up to Old Taggart which was another thing in New Taggart's s favor.

As I drove my old Chevy up the dusty mountain road leading to New Taggart on Monday evening I noticed the large stockpile of coal situated off to the left side of the road, with a large Hough end loader busily loading a 18 wheeler with coal to be transported to the Scotia tipple at the main mine site near the railroad tracks. Coal was pouring over the belt head and onto the stockpile of coal as I went by and was a pretty sight to even a new coal miner like myself. After all, extracting and moving the coal to market was what was paying our salaries and keeping us a good paying job.

As I pulled into the New Taggart parking lot I saw that the beltline from the mine ran across the edge of the parking lot. There was a wooden bridge or crosswalk built over the beltline so that miners could access the mine office and lighthouse which was located opposite the beltline from the parking area.

I walked across the crosswalk and as I did I could see that the mine office was located on a large flat with a large area dedicated to mining supplies, a large block building with three large rooms containing a lighthouse, a miner's waiting room, and a mine office. The building was about 24' by 48' in size.

There was no railroad tracks yet, as the mine wasn't advanced far enough, as I would find out when I went inside the mine for the first time. I wondered how the miners would get to the working face as I gazed at the four mine openings.

New Taggart consisted of four entries, from right to left, the mine fan entry, the beltline entry, the (soon to be) track entry, and the return entry. Over the next year and a half this would be my home away from home and I would come to know and even learned to (almost) love the place as well as anyone who worked there.

As I approached the building to report my presence I couldn't see a living person anywhere around the building or outside the mine. I had seen seven or eight vehicles in the parking lot so I knew at least some number of persons were either inside the mine or in the office building.

I stepped inside the office and saw no one was inside or anywhere around, it appeared. Opening the door to a much larger room, I saw a man lying on one of the wooden benches that were aligned along three walls of the building whom I had startled when I opened the door. He quickly jumped to his feet and exclaimed, "Come on in, I'm just resting my eyes until my men get here!"

I didn't know who I was addressing but I explained to him that I was sent here by the Upper Taggart second shift mine foreman and my boss, Sonny Cornett, and that I was looking for the mine foreman to report my presence. He laughed and said, "You're looking at the second shift mine foreman, the section foreman, the supply foreman, the belt man, and the maintenance foreman here at New Taggart! You're the first man here besides me, what's *your* name?" As he stood to shake my hand, I told him my name and with a grin he said, I'm Joe and I'm glad to meet you!"

I then explained that I had only been working as a miner two weeks and didn't yet know a lot about coal mining but I would do my best to make him a good work hand. He seemed pleased with those words and assured me that I'd do fine, that this was a new mine and his whole crew were still trying to "learn the ropes" here.

"You'll be my extra utility man on the section, I already have one man in that job but he needs a helper because right now the utility men have their hands full, having to shovel the beltline, keep the section clean and rock dusted, haul all the supplies inside, and help out in every way possible. You won't have time to be bored here!" I assured him I was ok with that and that I would do the best job for him I possibly could.

With the introductions and salutations out of the way he told me to check my man number tag on the board and asked me if I knew the reason for wearing the number on my belt too? I assured him that I knew that the tag on the board was for identifying who and how many men were inside the mine in case tragedy struck and the tag on the belt was for identifying the dead or badly injured that might occur in that event.

I grabbed a Wheat cap light from the light house, which was in fact just an adjoining room of the mine office and the check in/waiting room, and sat on one of the benches while waiting for the rest of the crew to arrive. One by one the other members of our crew began to arrive with their dinner buckets, water bottles and coats and jackets in their hands.

Underground coal mines have an average temperature of between 50 to 60 degrees Fahrenheit year round, which makes for a comfortable temperature inside the mine if one stays busy. Long sleeves and some type of jacket is a necessity for a miner unless the miner is a machine operator and the machine puts out enough heat to keep the operator warm.(When operating a piece of equipment I usually left my jacket in the dinner hole or somewhere around the section power center.)

When our crew gathered in the waiting room I saw that we numbered eleven men, including Joe, the boss. We varied in age from the early 20's to the late 50's as had been the case with my former crew mates at Upper Taggart. There were two utility men, of which I was one, two shuttle car operators, two bolting machine operators, a cutting machine operator, a loading machine operator, the coal drill operator, a repairman, and the Boss. All the crew were experienced miners (except me of course). Each of them had at least one year's underground experience and two or three of them had multiple years of coal mining to their credit.

Around 2:30 p.m. the dayshift crew came walking out the drift mouth at the mine entry straight across from the mining office. The men quickly went into the light house and put their lights on charge and with the banter common among coal miners all over the world, went over the beltline "bridge" to access their vehicles in the parking lot. Most of them would head for the bathhouse at the bottom of the hill while some would wait until they got home to take their bath.

When the day shift crew was all out of the mine and the day shift foreman had advised our boss of the working face conditions, Joe came out of the mine office and shouted, "Let's go boys, it's time to go to work!" With those encouraging words we started walking into the mine entrance with our dinner buckets and assorted paraphernalia in our hands.

A word about dinner buckets and drinking water here: most miners carried the square dinner buckets while usually some of the more experienced and older miners preferred the round dinner "pails" because those types of containers had a bottom compartment in which water could be carried, while the top half of the pail was reserved for food. While the square type bucket was pre-ferred by most Scotia miners, there was usually at least one in nearly every crew that carried the older style pails. I knew at least one miner that I later in my career worked with who carried an old quart Clorox bottle with his drinking water in it. At some point, around 1980 I believe, the company started furnishing drinking water for the miners, usually in eight ounce plastic bottles but sometimes in gallon plastic jugs. The water was distilled water which could also be used for watering the batteries on scoops and battery powered mantrip vehicles. This caused the gallon jugs to be more convenient and practi-cal to purchase. Keeping the water cold wasn't a problem since the temperature inside the mine was cool the whole year round.

That first day at New Taggart I found that this mine compared to the height of the coal in Upper Tag-gart was like the difference between daylight and dark-ness, New Taggart being the daylight and Upper Taggart being the darkness. I knew I was in a much better working environment the moment I stepped beyond the brattice cloth curtain stretched across the #2 entry, which was normally the track entry but there was no track laid there yet.(The one coal production section in the mine hadn't advanced far enough yet for track to be installed.)

I was surprised when I observed that the mine was more of a slope mine than a drift mine. It sloped at an angle of about 30% which made walking down the slope a little touchy because of the roof "sweating" and dripping water onto the bottom.4

Walking down the slope I judged the height of the mine to be around 72 to 80 inches, which was a world of difference compared to where I came from at Upper Taggart. Although I hadn't even seen the working face I was already convinced that I had reason to be thankful that I had been sent here instead of having to labor in conditions not very conducive to my or anyone else's good health.

After walking down the slope's seventeen breaks (approximately 1,500 feet,) we arrived on the section where I found the roof height there to vary between 55

---

4 In summer the air inside the mine cools and causes moisture to form on the roof of the mine which falls on the mine floor. In winter the air outside the mine warms as it enters and the moisture on the roof evaporates.

and 65 inches which was lower than I had expected because the slope was so high. Our section was only advanced about 200 feet from the bottom of the slope, making a total of nineteen breaks being driven since the mine was opened.

The mine bottom leveled off after that seventeen breaks of the slope and became more like a conventional drift mine. The only drawback was that the lower height after leveling off made standing or walking a little more difficult but not nearly as uncomfortable as I had experienced on the other side of the mountain. I found that I had to bend my neck nearly to my shoulders when standing or walking on section there. While this position was rough on the neck and shoulders the back had some relief from the strain of having to bend over and carry bags of rock dust and shoveling coal.

Most of the men on section were strangers to me although I had seen one or two of them around town or at other locations and though some of the names are part of my memory, others I don't remember so well. The fact that men were constantly being moved or transferred out of every mine section makes remembering them all difficult these many years later. Some that I do recall includes Glenn Abbott and Lester Holbrook, both of whom were shuttle car operators. The repairman was Danny

Adams, the loader operator was named ---- Spangler, the other utility man was ---- Holbrook, one of the bolting machine men was ---- Sexton. I do not recall the names of the cutting machine operator, the coal drill operator, nor can I recall bolting machine helper.

After arriving on section that first day, the boss sent the other utility man and me to shovel the feeder, and then instructed us to shovel the heading that the day shift had finished bolting at the end of their shift. All the cleaning and shoveling of the feeder and the ribs of all four mine headings had to be shoveled by hand, as there was no scoop available at our mine yet. That would only happen after the mine had advanced another few breaks or so.

Every mine supply we used had to be brought from the mine surface to the face area by way of a rubber wheeled vehicle called a "Julie car." This was a low, four tired tractor-like vehicle made of welded steel and used to transport men and supplies into and out of a mine. This vehicle had all-wheel steering and took some prac-tice to be able to safely and efficiently operate it. After a few weeks of riding shotgun with Holbrook while he and I carried supplies to the face area from the outside, I had finally mastered the intricacies of the steel monster and became fairly proficient in operating it.

It proved to be a good thing that I got the hang of it because about a month after I came on section Holbrook left for the day shift and the shoveling and supplying was all left in my hands. Not only was that job handed to me but since our section was a conventional section[5] I was tasked with helping the coal drill operator drill the holes in the coal, insert the powder sticks, and setting the charges off.

The coal drill operator had a unique relationship with the cutting machine operator. If the coal drill operator was slow in his job a fast cutting machine operator could keep well ahead in undercutting the coal for the coal drill operator to do his job.

On the other hand if the coal drill man was good and fast at his job or if he had a helper he could always catch up with the cutting machine man and relax on his machine until the coal was undercut. Almost every time I helped drill we ended up waiting as the cutting machine struggled to stay ahead of us.

While everyone on section carried on with jests and sometimes with horseplay I noticed that the cutter operator seemed to get more boisterous and agitated the more that I was assigned to help the coal drill man. This

---

[5] A conventional section uses a coal drill and blasting powder to loosen the coal at the face instead of a continuous mining machine, just like in the old days of mining.

wasn't helped when some of us had noticed before that the older man was possibly slightly inebriated at times which caused one of their playful arguments to escalate one day into a potentially dangerous situation.

I was again assigned to help the coal drill operator that day and when we once again caught up with the cutting machine the invariable playful joshing and ribbing began between the two operators. The cutting machine man was not at all happy that we had waited on him time and time again as he was sweating and hurriedly trying to get stay ahead of us. I could see that things were escalating when the two men began jawing and exchanging verbal jabs.

At one point they came close to each other and I saw the cutting machine operator reach in his front pocket and came out with a large knife. Opening it he began chasing the drill operator through the nearby breaks. I wasn't the only one who saw the incident but there were one or two others who happened to be around. The drill man being younger and faster he managed to keep well ahead of his antagonist and before long both men came back to the face area with no harm done.

Afterwards the incident was never mentioned again so I don't know if it was a planned event, a joke, or a serious situation that was thankfully ended without any harmful act being committed.

The men worked on this section many days after their flare-up without any problems and I don't know even at this date if it was all a farce or if the temporary anger exchange was real. The stress of the dangers involved in coal mining is real and is in many ways not unlike the PTSD which veterans suffer after serving in a combat zone. Having to watch the roof, ribs, and the movement of dangerous equipment in such cramped quarters every day in a coal mine tends to unnerve any otherwise sane man or woman.

CHAPTER FIVE

The stress factor not only played havoc in the mine but sometimes followed miners to their homes, as I found out one evening when I returned home after a hard shift at Scotia. Somehow our youngest son Jeffrey, who was then two years old, had wandered out of our front yard where he had been playing and just disappeared. I had returned home from work to find that Wanda had walked up the old mining road that ran in front of our house looking for him. The road turned uphill just past our house then ran for another quarter mile or so past a cemetery, then ran another thousand yards or to the top of the hill.

When I pulled in the driveway I heard Wanda shouting "Jeff! Jeff!" I could tell her voice was coming from somewhere on the old road that led to a worked out strip mine. I hurried up the road and saw Wanda coming down looking very pale and still shouting Jeff's name as she walked.

"What's the matter," I shouted. As I approached her I saw she'd been crying. "What's the matter?" "Oh Eddie, I can't find little Jeff!" She then explained that she had let Jeff play in the front yard and before she could turn around he had disappeared. We both hurried up the old road and checked the cemetery and surrounding area but found no sign of Jeff.

While Wanda went back off the hill to seek help in looking for Jeff, our then seven year old son Steve and Alisha, our five year old daughter, continued walking on up the road looking behind every tree and bush for him, to no avail.

Just a few minutes passed before Wanda and several young boys, some teenagers, some even younger, came up the hill and passed us heading for the old strip mine at the top of the hill to look for him. My two kids and I, along with Wanda, were still checking both sides of the road and behind the trees and bushes to make sure Jeff wasn't just playing hide-and-go-seek like children tend to do sometimes. As we traveled we shouted his name out hoping he might hear us but got no response in return.

As the teenagers returned from checking the old strip job for any sign of Jeff they assured us that they found no sign of him. Having checked everywhere we knew we decided to head down the hill and search behind our house and the surrounding area for any sign or for anything that might give us a clue as to where he might be. We were about to the point of calling in some more help when Wanda was standing in our front yard and screamed out "Jeff!" I was busy talking to someone about where we might look when Wanda's shout caused me to turn and see little Jeff walking down the road and babbling baby talk while sticking his finger in his mouth!

I'll never forget the sight he presented, with no clothing on his body except for his diaper and walking slowly down that road as if nothing was happening out of the ordinary. Wanda rushed up the road to grab him while sobbing and thanking God aloud for keeping him safe and bringing him home. I had rushed there behind Wanda and she and I, along with our other two kids just stood in the road with Jeff in our arms and hugged each other and thanked God together.

We never learned how we and all of the searchers missed seeing Jeff or where he was all that time. When we asked him where he was he didn't or couldn't say, but he would just point to the road going up the hill. Even today, 48 years later we still don't know how all those searchers managed to miss him or why he didn't answer when we shouted and hollered for him. The only theory I can come up with is that he might have fallen asleep on the hill and we missed him somehow.

By the time I had a been at New Taggart for a week or two I began to notice that since we were still mining so close to the outside that our boss Joe would make several trips outside during our shift. I assumed he was having a smoke since he would usually go outside with me and my other utility buddy and while we loaded up on supplies (which included cases of blasting powder,) he would smoke several cigarettes.

He would then send us back inside while he stayed outside for an hour or so while watching the coal pour over the beltline and into the stockpile. Just about all miners enjoy watching the coal they produce going into a stockpile where the trucks could be loaded with the coal. After all, coal is consider to be "black gold" and I imagine it is, because it eventually means more "gold" in the form of greenbacks for those engaged in mining and selling it.

Eventually Joe began spending more and more time on the outside while his crew was left to themselves for those longer periods of time. When questioned by some of the crew about his frequent absences he would just grin as he exclaimed, "I don't have to worry about you all because I can tell if you're working or not by the amount of coal coming over the belt!" He was correct in that assumption, as we were the only section in the mine at that time. Thankfully, all of his crew were fairly experienced miners, except for two or three of us and just about the whole crew were safety conscious miners.

One of the advantages of working on the second (or evening shift as some miners referred to it,) at New Taggart was that if one happened to be outside when the sun was going down you could observe some beautiful sunsets over the western mountain. While outside loading supplies I was fortunate to observe some of those beautiful sunsets from the Black Mountain peak that the New Taggart mine was located on. Being able to be outside at those times was worth the hard and dangerous labor we had to do in loading our mining supplies. The dangerous part was caused mostly by the blasting powder sticks and blasting caps we carried on our "Julie car."

After our foreman's trips to the outside of the mine became more frequent and at longer periods, those on the section began to be concerned that his actions could possibly result in his firing if he continued to spend so much time outside. After all, he was a very likeable guy and the crew respected his knowledge and his coal mining skills, which would account for nothing if he should lose his job or be transferred where he would be under the control of a higher mine authority.

Some of the crew actually at one point addressed him with their cautionary concern that his actions might well result in unfortunate consequences if he persisted in his behavior. They even mentioned to him that some thought he must be drinking something more than water while he was outside. They mentioned it in a vain as though they might be joking but in fact some of them had their suspicions. Their reason for concern was partly based upon the supposition that a different foreman might be a "hard driver" with a rougher nature than their present foreman. In any case they didn't want to exchange the known for the unknown.

About three or four months after I was transferred to New Taggart the fears of the Second shift crew were realized. Our foreman went out with me and my utility buddy to help us load mine supplies and after we completed the task he stayed outside as usual, saying, "You two go on back inside and I'll stay out here awhile so I can catch up on my paperwork."

We headed back inside with our load of supplies and headed back inside, traveling through the return entry as usual. A couple of hours later we got a call on the inner mine phone from the outside mine foreman at Upper Taggart. The repairman answered the phone and was informed that our own foreman had been "sent home."

He further related that a certified foreman was on the way up to our mine and would be walking inside shortly. At that time we still were having to walk in and out of the mine, because no steel railroad track had as of yet been installed inside our mine.

When we emerged from the drift mouth at the end of the shift the rumor among the third shift crew waiting to enter the mine was that our own foreman had been sent home by the higher ups. It seems that the guard stationed at the Scotia mine entrance had been making his rounds of checking all Scotia property during a shift and had found our boss "slightly inebriated" according to those same rumors. Whether true or not we never saw Joe again and regretted to see him go.

While our own crew had often joked among ourselves that John Barleycorn could be the reason he liked the outside so much none of us (to my knowledge) had seen any evidence to substantiate that rumor. I had been around him both inside and outside the mine and had never got a whiff of any strong drink when talking to him.

Regardless of the reason for his departure we all agreed that that he was good to the whole crew and the fact that he had a family to support made the situation that much worse.

CHAPTER SIX

J ack Begley was our new section foreman that would replace Joe. He would also usually help with loading supplies each time we made a trip outside, and he would always head back inside when we did. He did his share of the work and didn't ask us to do anything he wouldn't do himself including operating the equipment at the face to spell the regular operators out from time to time.

He once had me to operate one of our Joy 6SC shuttle cars while he operated the loader and the regular crew ate dinner at the power center. My having never operated a shuttle car before didn't bother him much. When I informed him I had never operated that piece of equipment before he quipped, "Oh, don't worry about it, you'll get the hang of it in no time."

He was slightly wrong about that. When I started the shuttle car and while Jack patiently waited at the controls of the loader, I proceeded to shear the nearby block of coal of about five foot of its rib. He was still watching me intently as I slowly backed up and started forward again only to shear another four or five feet from the previous block I had sheared.

I was determined to show him that I could in fact run anything on four wheels so I again backed the car out of the pile of coal I had knocked from the rib and proceeded to move forward and run into and over the brattice curtain that was run into the face to channel the fresh air to the face!

As I backed out I glanced up to see Jack vigorously shaking his cap light at me horizontally, which meant to "stop what you're doing." As I did so he shut the loader's motor down, climbed out of the loader operator's seat and with a sly grin said, "I believe we'd be better off to just wait until the loading crew finishes dinner!" I was in total agreement with him.

While unsuccessful at my first try as a shuttle car operator I would eventually master these "monsters of the deep" and would become a fairly proficient shuttle car operator for about twelve years or so of my mining career. The Joy 6SC cars used at New Taggart at that time had a capacity of only three tons which would be dwarfed by most of the shuttle cars I later operated, including large diesel shuttle cars we used in Scotia's #1 mine at a later date. If sideboards were installed were installed on the 6SC's (as they were on our section at that time) several more tons of coal could be held by them.

Although we had very good air inside the New Taggart mine the shoveling and rock dusting of the faces, breaks, and beltline had to be done by hand with #4 shovels for several months after the mine opened.

I still wore my dust mask around my neck and used it everywhere I went and with every task I did on section. It became my best friend because of the almost unbearable coal and rock dust created by the mining process. I would still nearly cough and gag my head off after I came outside the mine after a shift of breathing untold amounts of dust into my lungs. Some miners tolerated it better than others but any miner absorbs more than his share of the deadly dust despite the masks and ventilation measures to diffuse the dust.

Ironically, I would discover later that a coal section where coal is extracted by a continuous miner machine is more of a threat concerning dust hazards than a conventional section which uses a loader and blasts the coal from the face with dynamite. The reason for this is because "the continuous mining machine is a combined unit which produces all phases of operation: cutting, drilling, blasting, and loading; consequently the dust is accumulated in one mass and is released in one location."[6]

The storage of the explosives we used for blasting the coal from the face on section wasn't always possible to be exactly according the law and good common sense. Explosives were supposed to be stored on section in a dry place that was free from any danger of stray electric currents or from flying objects.

This wasn't always possible in an environment where water on the mine bottom was a normality on our section, especially in wintertime. I didn't know any better at the time because I hadn't yet seen a book on mining laws or received any classes on the subject, but most of the time blasting materials weren't carried on section in the correct manner. I guess good luck must have played a part in our safety measures because nothing out of the ordinary happened while our section operated as a conventional section.

As it was I spent a great deal of my time helping the coal drill man drilling, tamping, and wiring the powder charges in series to set off. We would drill five or six holes to a depth of about 10-12 feet, then insert between seven or eight sticks of powder, in one of which we in-

---

[6] Coal mining reference book; published by Kentucky Mining Institute, 1973.

serted a blasting cap, leaving the wire ends outside the hole to be wired in a series with the other holes. We would then tamp the sticks of powder gently but firmly with a wooden pole. Then after the wiring was completed two ends of the wiring were connected to a roll of 100' insulated wire and that cable was then connected to a shooting battery. Then either the coal drill man or I, as his helper, would holler three times, Fire! Fire! Fire! Then push the button which would set off the charges.

If the charges were set correctly a sizeable cut of coal would then be available for the loader man to load into the shuttle cars. The loader we used was a Joy 11 BU loader, which could load approximately five tons a minute. Our shuttle cars with their sideboards could hold five tons easily but sometimes the mine roof would be low enough to sweep some of the coal onto the mine floor as the car traveled to the feeder to dump the coal. Since we didn't yet have a scoop to do the job I had to clean up the spills by means of a #4 shovel, sometimes with the help of the shuttle car operators.

On November 1st, 1974, Scotia underground employees received a $3.00 per shift increase per their 1973 contract. This brought my pay as an inside utility man to $49.46 per shift. This daily pay if calculated with inflation factors considered would now be worth $260.66.

Our contracts with Scotia were always negotiated in three year increments and the pay increases were always listed as increases in per shift pay instead of being broken down into hourly increases. Those miners classified as "inside" miners were paid slightly more than those miners classified as "outside" employees. The contract for 1982 will provide an example here:

At the top of the pay scale were the continuous miner operators, first class repairmen, first class electricians, belt repairmen, and roof bolter operators at $102.00 per shift.

Just below the top pay scale were the loader operators, cutting machine men, and the cutting machine helpers at $101.68 per shift.

Next were the roof bolt helpers, driller and shooter, and sectional utility whose pay was $100.46 per shift.

Second class repairmen, second class electricians, brakemen, coal drillers, trackmen, timbermen, bratticemen, wiremen and bonders, shot firers, loading point men, and beltmen were earning $99.25 per shift.

Shuttle car operators, motor men, rock drillers, and radio and telephone repairmen received $99.44 per shift.

Track helpers, timber helpers, bratticemen helpers, water pumpers, supplymen, and general inside miners were compensated at the least of the pay scale for inside work at $98.96 per shift.

You might have noticed that the pay scales listed refer to *men* at the end of some of the jobs. This was likely a carryover from the old days when only men were miners. At the date of the 1982 contract just cited a very few women miners were employed at Scotia but their numbers were increasing slightly nearly every year and their pay was the same as the men when the woman were doing the same job.

Those miners classified as outside workers earned even less except for a few categories of skilled outside workers, such as Electricians, plumbers, carpenters, and heavy equipment operators who earned just a few cents more per shift than the lowest paid inside miners.

In January 1975 Jack Begley was either transferred to another mine or went to work for another company and Veril Boggs was transferred from another mine to New Taggart and became our new section foreman.

He also held the title of second shift mine foreman by reason of being the only foreman on the second shift because ours was the only section then in operation at that date.

Veril was a genuine "mover and shaker" and seemed to have a knack of getting things done when he set his mind to it. Our section had by then advanced far beyond the point they were at when I was transferred there in September 1774. The walk inside and hauling supplies from the outside was beginning to take up a lot of time just traveling back and forth. Sometimes we would have to make several trips to the outside in the "Julie car" to get a needed part or supplies which caused delays in production.

We had asked for some track to be installed so we could make quicker trip and get the men to the working section quicker, but for some reason the rails hadn't been delivered yet. Veril somehow got the ball rolling and shortly after he arrived, a load of 60# steel rails were delivered to our supply yard at New Taggart.

Instead of waiting until the track crew could work our mine into their schedule, Veril took charge and our crew began "doubling back" after our regular shift and worked on installing the rails ourselves. In just a few days we had the thirty three foot long rails laid all the way to our section inside the mine.

Our Julie car was now obsolete and very soon it was sitting outside the mine to be picked up by a crew and taken to parts unknown. I can't say that I missed it very much, as the return entry we used to make our trips in that vehicle was so muddy and slick that the trips outside were becoming more than a hindrance than a help to us.

In a few days a truck brought us a bright yellow 6 ton locomotive and a couple of supply cars to use in hauling our supplies and men into and out of the mine. Unlike the 5 ton track motors being used at Middle Taggart (B seam) and Upper Taggart, our 6 ton motor was powered by two electric batteries which were much more convenient. The motors in the middle and upper mines were operated using poles hooked to an electric line of 400 volts which was installed overhead on one side of the mine all the way through the mine.

An accidental touching, grabbing, or falling against that electric line could mean a quick death or serious injury to the unlucky or careless miner that somehow got into the wire's current. Battery powered rail equipment made that event much more unlikely of occurring.

With the addition of the track and motor my duties increased substantially. Not only was I responsible for my section's supplies, shoveling the ribs, the feeder tailpiece, and running the new motor, but I also had to help the repairman and the bolting machine operator while I had any "free time." Naturally I never had any of that free time but had to help anyway.

Eventually Veril made me his permanent motor-man and replaced me on section with another utility man., making my life a little less complex in the mine. I still had to help out at the face when needed though.

While still working at the face and helping the coal drill operator drill and shoot, we had a close call at one point. We drilled the holes in the coal and tamped the powder charges in a right hand break we had turned and were advanced about seventy feet into the break, which left only about 10 or 12 feet of coal to be blasted out. After setting the charges we rolled our firing cable around the corner of the break until reaching the end of the 100 foot firing cable, and then the drill man attached the cable to the firing battery.

He shouted out the required "Fire! Fire! Fire!" then set the blast off. A few seconds later we observed two figures emerging out the smoke and dust of the #4 entry that the shot we put off was trying to blast through! We rushed to them to make sure they were alright and they assured they were ok except for a few pits from fine coal to the face and their caps blown off their heads.

Without our knowledge two engineers setting spads[7] had walked into the adjoining break and had been

---

[7] A metal spad was hammered into the mine roof to align the direction of the cuts of coal.

63

just a few feet away from the coal that the blast exited. Luckily a tragedy had been avoided but we never knew why no one informed us that the engineers were on section setting spads. Although badly shaken they weren't seriously injured from the blast.

A few days later in June 1975, Veril Boggs' nephew Kenneth Boggs was killed in an accident involving the shuttle car he was operating. The car's canopy caught him against the coal rib, resulting in his death. I was standing near Veril that evening on section when he received the call from the mine dispatcher that his nephew had been hurt.

Kenneth's accidental death was the first in the Scotia mine since 1971 when utility man Dale Cornett was killed by a rib roll. Dale's death resulted in a $5,500 fine for Scotia for their "failure to detect and take down or adequately support a loose overhanging brow," according to Federal Investigators who faulted management for that failure.

CHAPTER SEVEN

With the track rails now installed a new section was turned off a few breaks from the bottom of the slope in New Taggart and a new crew was placed there to drive that section. Some men from Upper Taggart were sent to man the new section which would be the first continuous miner section at New Taggart. Eventually the coal drill, cutting machine, and loading machine on the original section of New Taggart was exchanged for their own continuous mining machine.

I was involved in moving all the new (to that mine) equipment into the mine along with a new man that was sent to run a five ton low vane motor that joined the six ton motor I had been operating. With two new sections added and when the third shift crew is counted at this point there were at least fifty men now working on the two sections at New Taggart. We motormen were kept busy supplying the two sections and rock dusting the four mine entries all the way to the headings of both working sections.

Our job rock dusting the mine was made much easier by the addition of a two ton rock duster machine on rails that Veril Boggs asked for and received from mine management. My motor co-worker and I doubled back after our shift was over several times a month and rock dusted the mine. It was much easier to complete that operation since mine traffic was lower on the third shift, so we took advantage to rock dust on that shift.

Another advantage of third shift rock dusting was that there were far fewer men working on the third shift crews to have to breathe the dust we were blowing into the air intake entries. We always wore our dust masks but they were very little help in keeping the dust from out of our respiratory system.

A fifty foot long four inch diameter hose was attached to the duster so the dust could be scattered into nearly all the entries. We eventually added another fifty feet to the hose which enabled us to reach all the entries from the track up to the sections.

Shortly after we got the new duster Veril Boggs was transferred to another Scotia mine and Jerry Herrin arrived at New Taggart as the new second shift mine foreman. He left the Upper Taggart mine where my other brother Philip had been working as a belt man.

Phil had put his application in with the State Police at the same time he had applied for a job with Scotia. About six months after hiring on with Scotia he had received a call from the Kentucky State Police advising him that he had been accepted as a cadet at the Academy. He decided to accept their offer and left Scotia to become a successful State Trooper, retiring after 20 years in the job. He later worked as a Whitesburg, Kentucky city policeman before he passed away with cancer in 2004.

After Phil left Scotia, Jerry, who had been Phil's boss at Upper Taggart, told me that Phil was the best belt head man he had seen, that he was the only man on that particular belt that had cleaned it so well of coal muck that one could eat off the bottom. He asked me to tell Phil that he was welcome back to Scotia and his old job any time he wanted it. That was high praise from Jerry.

It seemed that none of the outside mine foremen lasted for very long in that job for various reasons, usually to move a little higher on the rung. So was it with Jerry, who left New Taggart after the explosions of March 9 and 11, 1976, to captain one of the rescue teams Scotia formed and trained after those tragedies. (I'll have more to say about these tragedies in other chapters of this book.)

With the departure of Jerry, Bruce Jones was elevated to second shift mine foreman. Bruce had come from Upper Taggart a short time before to be Jerry's assistant mine foreman.

Bruce was one of my favorite people, soft spoken and very personable. He was able to get along with anybody and everybody and was respected by everyone he came in contact with at Scotia. He was never one to blame someone else for any failures that might occur around him, but would quickly take the blame for his men's mistakes or failures on his own shoulders.

When shoveling a beltline or rock dusting the mine he worked as hard if not harder than his men, earning their respect in the effort. He would not send men to do a tough job without going with them and joining in the effort to do the job, whether it was a large area of water that had to be pumped to the outside or a rock fall that had to be cleaned up, he was there and actively involved in the work. He knew how to get things done.

In the latter part of 1975 Scotia workers received an unexpected $10.00 per shift raise. With the raise my pay was then $59.46 per shift which was $10.00 per shift above what our contract called for. While the reason for the raise wasn't known for sure, a government contract for coal was cited by some for the reason. Some others suspect that Scotia's parent company, Blue Diamond, was around that same time found guilty of ignoring minimum wage and safety laws in violation of the *Walsh-Healy Public Contracts Act*.

Another coal mining section was soon started in the New Taggart mine, which resulted in adding an additional twenty five or more men to work on that section in the three eight hour shifts. Our motor crew gained an additional helper because of the added supplies needed and the extra rock dusting required with the addition of the new section. More heavy equipment needed to be hauled into the mine also and the extra man was badly needed to help on the motors as the motormen sometimes were drafted to help on one of the sections when a member of their regular crew was absent.

Anytime a group of men are placed together in a working situation, a lot of wise-cracking words, ribbing, and horse playing eventually takes place and nearly all coal miners are notorious for such antics. Usually the acting the fool is accepted with good humor by the one on the receiving end of the barbs and retaliation usually ends with laughter all around.

Unfortunately one of my co-workers wasn't in the mood for slapstick antics one cold day and a verbal altercation quickly escalated into an angry exchange of blows that I attempted to deescalate and get between them, to no avail. The fight continued for a couple of minutes then ended by mutual agreement, but things were never the same afterwards and our new helper ended up being transferred to the Upper Taggart mine.

The fracas was never mentioned again by anyone to my knowledge but it's likely that our boss, the New Taggart second shift foreman, somehow heard of the disagreement between my two co-workers and tried to diffuse the situation before real problems were encountered, by removing the newer man. I had always gotten along with both men and regretted their not being able to get along with each other. Instead of having an extra man to help on the sections and with handling supplies we were again shorthanded as a motor crew.

A close call was experienced by our two man motor crew one day when our locomotive was attached to a couple of empty supply cars as we headed outside the mine. We had a hill we had to go down and as it was, that part of the mine was the lowest of all New Taggart mine roofs.

I was riding shotgun while my buddy was operating our six ton battery motor as we started down the steep hill. We had to lower our heads and ride down the hill blindly due to the low roof and couldn't see the supply cars we were pushing ahead of us. Somehow the coupling on one of the cars came loose which let the supply cars rush down the hill we were traveling, only to stop a short distance ahead, causing us to plow into the three ton supply cars as we traveled very fast down the hill with the six ton motor.

When we collided (more of a crash) we both thought we had met another locomotive coming into the mine. We had not yet realized that our supply cars had come uncoupled. The collision knocked our hats and lights off our heads, my hat and attached light actually falling just under the deck of the locomotive. We were both temporarily stunned with the force we had just absorbed and confused with what had just happened. After a few minutes of reorienting ourselves we again coupled the supply car to our motor and proceeded outside, chastened and vowing that we would use safety chains with the couplings in the future.

Mine laws are made for a reason, usually after a disaster has occurred and for some unknown reason at this late date we failed to attach a locomotive to each end of the supply cars like the regulations specified. We were both usually safety conscious motormen so there was likely a good reason for our neglect for which I can't recall at this point in time.

As we entered the winter months of late 1975 we were reminded to be extra careful because of the changing mine conditions that occur with the onset of winter.

Since most gas explosions, dust explosions, and mine fires resulting in disaster occur during the fall and winter, a watchful eye concerning the barometric pressure readings became necessary in cold weather.

When the barometric pressure falls due to a cold front moving in, the mine atmosphere and mine surfaces are usually drier. When that event occurs, an increase in methane liberation from above and below the coal bed, gob and abandoned areas, and from the rock strata, increases the danger of fires and/or explosions.

The increased liberation of methane during the cold season is because of the fact that the colder air being pulled into the mine is warmed by the warmer temperature inside the mine and as the air is warmed it picks up the moisture from mine surfaces and exhausts it to the outside. The drier conditions left inside the mine by this action results in drier mine surfaces and drier coal dust, resulting in extra dangerous working conditions due to the increased danger of fire or explosion.

One of the best means of preventing explosions and fire inside the mine in all seasons is through the use of plenty of rock dust inside the mine. Another good preventive is to make sure methane checks are made frequently along with oxygen level checks.

I know from experience that sparks from metal tools striking against sandstone or some other hard rock will cause sparking that can result in ignition of even a pocket of methane. Many experienced coal miners have observed what happens when the continuous miner bits hits a sandstone and a pocket of methane, causing the bits to spark the sandstone and ignite the methane, causing a loud blast and flame shooting from the face of the coal. The first time one experiences this is fairly disturbing as it shows that methane is present, albeit in a small and harmless amount as long as there is plenty of fresh air flowing across the face of the cut of coal.

On January 16, 1975, one of our local newspapers, _The Mountain Eagle,_ reported that twenty coal miners lost their lives in Kentucky coal mines in 1974, a record low number.

CHAPTER EIGHT

One cold day and snowy afternoon in January, 1975, I headed up the north side of Pine Mountain, (elevation 2,400 ft.) and found the going a little slick but not too difficult for my Chevy station wagon to negotiate, even though a few light snow flakes were falling and sticking to the road. As I started down the south side of the mountain, I could see the snow covered Black Mountains which towered over the Poor Fork valley floor. The scene was beautiful and would have been very inspiring and ideal for an artist to paint the scene at that moment.

What was not a beautiful and inspiring sight was the large eighteen wheeler semi I met in a curve as he was coming up the south side of the mountain. I had no choice but to put my '69 Chevy directly into the ditch line, which had three inches or more of snow in it and the snow was still peppering down. He had his side of the road and over half of mine, as the saying went.

The truck continued on up the mountain having missed hitting me by inches even though my car was cocked sideways in the ditch. I didn't blame the truck driver then or now. If he had stopped to apologize or try to help he would have never been able to pull out and proceed up the mountain without the assistance of a wrecker or chains on his tractor.

The narrow two lane road which wound up the mountain on both the north and south side was barely suitable for two cars to pass in places, much less an eighteen wheeler truck. I came upon many accidents and vehicles stranded in the ditch lines of that storied mountain during my years of traveling over that ten miles of narrow road during my more than seventeen years at Scotia but that was the first and last time I had to put my vehicle in the ditch while crossing the mountain.

I grabbed my dinner bucket and jacket from the car and waited until another Scotia worker came by and gave me a lift to the Scotia bath house. I can't remember who the miner was that picked me up that day since it happened over 46 years ago.

Many Scotia workers lived on the north side of that mountain in Letcher and the adjoining counties of Perry, Knott and Pike, all of which had at least a handful of Scotia employees living there. A steady line of their vehicles were sure to come along heading to and coming from the Scotia mine when the shifts at Scotia changed.

Later that night after my shift at Scotia was over my brother Jimmy gave me a ride home. As we traveled up the south side of the mountain we observed that the snow cover of the afternoon was now gone. The temperature had risen above freezing and melted most of the snow on Pine Mountain.

As we came to the curve where I expected to find my vehicle in the ditch I was surprised to see that it was gone! Jimmy and I speculated that either it had been stolen or a family member or friend had managed to get it out of the ditch. I had called my wife from the Scotia bath house and explained my predicament in case someone recognized my car in the ditch and informed her about the situation.

In those days there were no cell phones to carry around on our persons. We communicated with home by way of Citizen Band radios, (c. b. radios for short) and Jimmy had one in his Volkswagen which we used to call my home when we discovered my car gone from the ditch. We had waited to cross over the top on the mountain and we going down the north side of the mountain to call my home. This was necessary because the reception was spotty and nearly non-existent on the far side of the mountain making the signal weak and difficult to communicate between parties.

It seems kind of silly these days, having to shout into a car's C.B. microphone, "Green Machine to base, Green Machine to base, can you hear me?" In a few moments and with some annoying interference and much screeching I heard my wife's voice saying, "Green Machine base to mobile Green Machine, got you loud and clear, 10-4?"

This was the latest in technology and although this way of communication seems crude today it worked and saved time and money in the process. I once left my mining boots and my dinner bucket sitting on the porch of my home in Colson and was going through Thornton Gap when I received a call from my wife telling me of my blunder.

I immediately turned around and retrieved the much needed items and still had plenty of time to get to work since I always left at least an hour and a half before work time in case I might have trouble of some kind getting to work. My old Chevy was somewhat unpredictable and unreliable after so many trips across Pine Mountain by that point in time.

I should here confess that I was still wearing my house shoes when she called me that day about leaving my mining gear on the porch. I don't believe it's necessarily true that only professors are absent minded. I can vouch that coal miners sometimes claim that title.

After my wife answered my call she told me that after I called her from the bath house she had called my dad, who had then asked a family member to take him on the mountain to see what he had to do to retrieve my stranded Chevy. She related to me that he said he had just climbed into the car, started it up and managed to just drive it down the ditch and climb slowly onto the highway, saving me a tow bill.

I was surprised and a little embarrassed to hear that he had just driven the car out of the ditch on its own without needing to pull it out. I was also very thankful to have a dad who was always handy to have around because of being so level headed in times of distress.

On one occasion when I was about seven years old our family was traveling through the old Carr's Fork road in Knott County and came upon a bad auto wreck where a car had gone over the hill and turned over. An injured man was lying on the side of the road and several people were milling around and talking among themselves instead of rendering aid to the injured man. He didn't have any visible injuries on him but was unconscious and no one in the crowd seemed to know what to do or when to do it.

My dad was not one to be indecisive, so when he came up to where the man was lying, he quickly checked the man for a pulse, and saw that he had a pulse and was breathing normally. He then headed for our old car and retrieved a quilt he used to cover the seats when hauling fellow miners back and forth to work when it was his time to share a ride.

Rushing back to the unconscious man he spread the quilt over the man and continued his ministrations to the man, trying to make him comfortable as possible. As he did so, someone in the hovering crowd spoke up and said, "Folks, please back away from the doctor and let him in here to do his job!" My dad looked around to see the doctor only to see that people were staring at *him,* thinking he was a doctor. He then realized that he had on a white shirt and a white pair of pants, looking very much like he was wearing a doctor's hospital attire.

We stayed there until the ambulance came and picked the man up from the side of the road and whisked him away from the scene. My dad then retrieved his old car seat quilt and we continued on our way to Granny's house on Tunnel Hill, in Letcher County, with the coal miner "doctor" at the wheel!

My mom needled him relentlessly for years after that incident and would say that he was the only doctor she ever saw that made his living working in a coal mine. He always took any kidding directed towards him with a grain of salt, not getting angry, but enjoying humor directed at him along with the one telling the funny story.

He really was "one of a kind," having started working in a coal mine at fourteen years of age after having quit school after completing the fourth grade. He was blessed with plenty of common sense though, working as a coal miner and a carpenter until Pearl Harbor when the army called him up for duty in the Pacific theater. He received his driver's license at the age of fourteen when his dad bought a car to haul miners back and forth to work. In those days no test was required, just pay for the license and you were authorized to drive anything as long as you could see over the steering wheel and maneuver the vehicle around.

When my old Chevy became more unreliable I ended up giving the car to my dad who drove it several years before it finally gave out. He used it to haul his grandchildren around the area when they needed to go somewhere. Once he had several of them loaded into the Chevy and a couple of them were riding in the back of the old station wagon with the back window rolled down. They were having a good time chatting and gazing out the open back window while moving along the old road up Thornton creek.

As the car slowed, they came upon a group of youngsters about their age when Jimmy's daughter Merenda, who was one of the girls who were sitting at the back window, saw their friends staring at the old Chevy wagon as they passed by. Merenda felt a little ashamed of being seen in the old dusty Chevy by her friends, so she quickly hung her head out the window and shouted to them "This isn't our car! This isn't our car!" I don't know if she convinced any of them of that fact though. Riding in the back with the rear window rolled down had been fun until friends from school saw them, causing them to be embarrassed by the dust covered Chevy.

At one point after I gave the Chevy to my dad and I rode with Jimmy to the mine for a few weeks in his black Volkswagen car which was much cheaper on gas than my Dodge truck. For several years afterward I would kid him about letting his Volkswagen coast off Pine Mountain to save gas. I don't remember now if that really happened or if I was joking at the time. Either way it fit Jimmy's conservative nature when it comes to finances and it makes for a good memory of our Scotia mining days.

By the end of 1975 the New Taggart mine had added another couple of working sections which made the parking lot pretty full during the day and evening when coal was being produced. Normally no coal was produced during the third shift but occasionally one section or two would "double back" and produce coal for an additional few hours before the day shift arrived.

Our mining contract called for time and a half for all time worked over eight hours, so the incentive to work overtime was strong. The good part about that was that I don't recall management ever asking the employees to limit their overtime. The fact is that they encourage it but didn't demand anyone work if they didn't want to. If overtime was needed to complete a new project or make a belt or section move, most miners were willing to work when asked to by management. The employees were making very good money and most, if not all of them, appreciated the work.

Inspections were carried out frequently at Scotia mines, both the Upper Taggart, New Taggart, and at the main #1 Scotia mine in the Imboden seam of coal. One of the inspections of the main #1 mine resulted in a 104B Closure Order on October 22, 1975 which the Pikeville, Kentucky office of the Mining Enforcement and Safety Administration (MESA) accused them on Oct. 23 of ignoring the order. Below is the letter in part;

To: Lawrence D. Phillips, District Manager, Coal Mine Health and Safety District 6
From: Ronald D. Suttles, Federal Mine Inspector

Subject: 104B Closure Order at the Scotia Mine, Scotia Coal Company, Oven Fork, Letcher County, Kentucky.

October 22, 1975 I issued 104B Order, No. 1 RDS, 75-1710, on the cabs and canopies, at 9:45 a.m. on the National Mine Service Torkars (shuttle cars) that includes each coal producing section at the mine.

October 23, 1975, I arrived at the Scotia Mine, new return airway section to the surface. At 8:30 a.m. I observer coal coming out on the main belt, which transports coal from the five sections underground at the main mine. At 9.00 a.m. I talked with Charles Kirk, Safety Inspector. I informed Mr. Kirk that Scotia was working under an order. Mr. Kirk made no comment. I left Scotia Coal Company at 9:15 a.m. Coal was still being dumped from the belt conveyor, new return airway section 025-0.

Arrived back at the office 10:00 a.m.

Ronald D. Suttles
Federal Coal mine Inspector

A 104 (B) Closure was not an imminent danger Closure Order, although Scotia was issued nine 104 (A) Closure Orders in 1975.

CHAPTER NINE

The Scotia mine was started in 1962 by the Blue Diamond Coal Company of Knoxville, Tennessee. The mine was located near Oven Fork, Letcher County, Kentucky on the Poor Fork of the Cumberland River, which is approximately 14 miles northeast of Cumberland, Harlan County, Kentucky. The distance from the county seat of Letcher County, Whitesburg, is approximately 15 miles.

In 1963 the Louisville and Nashville (L&N) railroad extended a branch of their line from Cumberland, Kentucky to the Scotia mining complex, which was just over 14 miles in distance.

The coal reserves Scotia would be mining was mostly of high quality metallurgical coal for steel making and for electricity producing power plants. Scotia's new mine was timely because the year 1963 was when the unit train loading system was introduced to large coal producing mines. These unit trains usually averaged 100 gondolas of 100 tons capacity each which could be loaded in just a few hours without ever uncoupling from the locomotive pulling the unit train.

In June, 1966, Scotia miners went on strike after the majority of the workers voted for United Mine Workers representation but by June, 1967 the strike ended with the failure to organize the workers. In 1969 the Scotia miners formed their own union called The Scotia Employees Union (S.E.U.) which was successful and lasted as long as Scotia lasted.

When Scotia opened the #1 Imboden mine in 1962 they opened several openings in that seam of coal which was located at the foot of Big Black Mountain in Oven Fork, Kentucky. In the early 1970's they opened two more mines higher up the mountain, Upper Taggart and Middle Taggart mines. Upper Taggart was also known as Old Taggart and Middle Taggart was also known as the B Seam. In early 1974 they opened the New Taggart mine across the ridge from Old Taggart.

This made a total of four different mining complexes which were in production at the same time by the year 1975. The Scotia #1 mine at the bottom of the mountain was a sloped or inclined mine of four original entries and eventually a new entry was mined for the slope track and the #2 airway entry.

Unlike the bottom mine the three upper mines were drift mines with varying height of the coal seam. The B seam was the lowest coal at between 38 and 45 inches, the Upper Taggart mine varied from 42 to 52 inches, and the New Taggart being between 55 to 60 inches in height. The main #1 mine had coal height between 6 ft. to 7 ft. Height.

The #1 mine had some soft shell spots in the mine roof which had a tendency to slough between the roof bolts in the entries closer to the outside. A roof bolter machine, from time to time, had to be transported to the old entries leading from the main outside in the #1 mine to install new roof bolts. Usually the new bolts had to be of at least ten foot length in order to reach the roof ceiling because of the rock falling from between the old bolts and leaving gaps in the rock.

After the twin explosions in 1976, I helped install a number of those bolts near the mine entrance and even with a ten foot bolt one had to stand on the bolter safety canopy in order to reach the hole that was drilled. This wasn't the safest thing in the world to do but the only other choice would have been to let some of the mine roof cave in and that really wasn't an option.

In 1975, a bore hole was drilled at Frank's Creek in order to shorten the distance between the main mine and the Northeast works of the Scotia mine. The distance to those sections was over five miles from the main Scotia complex (even further by highway from the main mine) but the new opening made the distance only a few hundred feet away from the new entrance to the north-east workings.

The bore hole opening was 13 and ½ foot in diameter and 376 foot deep. The shaft was lined with concrete by July 21, 1975 and an electric elevator was to be installed. When the mine suffered the first explosion on March 9, 1976 the elevator entrance hadn't yet been completed.

At the end of 1975 Scotia had 314 employees working at the main #1 mine, with six sections, five continuous miner sections and one conventional section. All together those six sections produced about 2,500 tons of coal daily.

The three upper Black Mountain mines had five sections and produced a little less tonnage than did the #1 mine. These mines (New Taggart, B Seam, and Upper Taggart) had 225 employees at the end of 1975.

Safety Hazards at Scotia

Safety hazards at Scotia differed very little from the things encountered in other large coal mines throughout the United States. The upper Black Mountain coal producing sections in particular had minor safety issues compared with the #1 main mine of Scotia because of the higher coal and problems with the slate roof and especially with the methane issue.

The Imboden seam of coal in the bottom mine was beneath the water table which resulted in a great amount of methane being emitted from the roof, coal, ribs, and gob piles in the mine. This Scotia mine liberated between 200,000 and 500,000 cubic feet of methane per 24 hours, according to a government staff report.

This same report states that at various times methane readings in the bottom mine registered as high as nine percent. Kentucky mine laws required a check for methane should be made every 20 minutes while electric equipment is operating at the face. In the bottom mine most miners did their best to make sure regular methane checks were made at the required 20 minute intervals but the same staff report said that this regulation was regularly violated and seldom adhered to at the Scotia mine.

The upper Scotia mines were above the water table and had little problem with elevated methane readings when producing coal at the face or even out by the face area. I personally don't remember ever getting a positive methane reading while operating a scoop and taking a required 20 minute reading while cleaning the ribs and rock dusting a face area at New Taggart.

A common problem in the bottom mine was getting enough air flow across the face of the coal to achieve the required 9.000 cubic feet per minute in order to cut the coal. A great deal of production time was taken up in just trying to get the minimum air needed. The mine had progressed so far from the original 1962 openings that the distance from the mine fans and air intake entries, the numerous gob piles, falling rock, broken stoppings, etc., made ventilation difficult to achieve. The 2 Southeast Mains heading was about 4 and ½ miles from the main complex, causing proper ventilation difficult at times because of the large area the mine fan had to provide fresh air for.

After Scotia suffered the twin explosions in 1976 and the mine recovery was underway, two new coal production sections were started near the area of the first explosion, in order to create two new airways. I worked on one of those sections in the late 70's as a shuttle car operator. We were told by supervisors that there was some sense of urgency to get those airways created in order to solve the ventilation problems in the bottom mine. The completion of those airways did indeed greatly improve ventilation in the Scotia #1 mine in the last years of its operation.

The three other mines of Scotia didn't have to worry too much about adequate ventilation but water on some sections and the low coal created their own problems. The Upper Taggart mine as I stated before, used the trolley system to operate their 5 and 6 ton locomotives.

The trolley systems are the simplest type of electrical circuit in mining. There are two main conductors, the feed wire and the return. The trolley feed wire is installed on insulators. The steel tracks are the return conductors and are grounded. To operate a trolley-powered locomotive, the locomotive is connected with one wire to the tracks, through the wheels. Pumps and section equipment are connected in the same way but through more permanent electrical connections.

A voltage of 300 to 600 volts is present between the trolley wire and the track. Anyone working on an energized wire and standing on a rail without proper insulated gloves and shoes would be subject to electrocution.

Trolley wires were required to be 6 & ½ feet above the mine floor or guarded where men are required to pass under the wire or work nearby regularly. Guarding is also required where personnel board or disembark from personnel carriers, called man trip stations, and at the beginning and end of trolley wires. Trolley wire guards are usually yellow plastic or vinyl (as they were at Upper Taggart) that enclose the bare ungrounded wire. Guards are used to prevent electrocution due to accidental contact.[8]

No way did the Upper Taggart mine conform to the regulation the trolley wire was to be 6 & ½ feet above the mine floor, which was impossible when the mine roof was less than five foot in height in most places. Although they did conform to the regulation by guarding the trolley wire where men were required to pass under or work near the wire regularly.

Many Scotia miners have experienced what it is like to accidently touch the wire with one's body or rescuer which hung from the mining belt. Even if the miner is wearing rubber boots he can sometimes receive a shock when accidently touching the wire. Some of the braver (or crazier) miners would touch the wire on purpose while wearing gloves and rubber boots while standing on the steel rails in an act of boastful showmanship. Fortunately those I observed managed to safely accomplish the "trick."

Arcs in electrical circuits cause 80 percent of electrical injuries. One source of exposed arcing is the trolley

---

[8] U.S. Department of Labor. Mine Health and Safety Administration Safety Manual # 9.

wires and connections to trolley wires. When a cable had to be connected to a bare trolley wire a "fuse nip" was used A fuse nip is a fiber-type cylinder with a fuse inside, a copper hook attached to one end and a power conductor to the other.

Many Scotia miners can remember working at Upper Taggart and when the motor operator got ready to move the motor into the mine he would touch the nip to the wire, causing an arc that resembles a welding arc. Looking directly at the nip arc could have resulted in an eye injury. The correct maneuver was to turn your head slightly to the side and touch the back of the hook to the wire to see if it causes an arc. If no arc was detected it was safe to place the nip hook on the wire.

Thankfully those of us that worked at New Taggart as motormen missed most of the aggravation that trolley motormen have to endure, especially in the low roof of Upper Taggart and the B Seam. Watering the batteries and having to put those batteries on charge occasionally when using battery powered motors was much easier and simpler for those of us who operated the motors of New Taggart.

Operating or helping on a bolting machine was one of the more dangerous jobs on a coal mining section due to having to work under supported top to set jacks before bolting a heading after a cut of coal had been removed. Resin bolts were installed on four foot centers and steel screw type jacks had to be set before bolting could be done. A bolter helper had no canopy to protect him or her when they stepped 4 feet ahead of the last row of bolts to set jacks before bolting the roof.

The danger of bolting the top in the mines was made clear to me once when I was present when a bolting machine operator was mortally injured while setting a jack where he was preparing to bolt a place the continuous miner had just cleaned up. Our production crew, including the roof bolter operator, had just got off the mantrip a few minutes before it happened.

I got on my shuttle car to get a load of coal in the #2 entry and as I approached the #3 entry I saw the bolter parked just in by that open break and noticed his bolting machine cable was stretched across the entry and he was flagging me to stop. Running over any electric cable, especially a shuttle car cable, a bolter cable, or a miner cable was a no-no and could be a firing offence, depending on whether it was an accidental, through negligence, or a deliberate act.

After I stopped my shuttle car I got out of the car and helped the bolting machine operator hang his cable across the break so I could proceed with my car to the #

2 heading where the miner operator was waiting to load my shuttle car. After helping hang his bolting machine cable to a roof bolt I saw he had been setting his jacks in the heading of #3 where the continuous miner had moved from. I grabbed a roof jack from the top of the roof bolter and carried it to the cleaned up cut and stepped four feet from the last row of bolts and set the jack I had retrieved from the roof bolter. Nearby, the section repairman was watching us as we set the two jacks. Seeing that all the jacks were set but one and the bolting man picking it up to set, I proceeded around the corner to get back on my shuttle car to get a load of coal.

As I climbed into the operating deck of the car, I heard the repairman who had been observing us holler out, "Eddie, go call outside, C----- is killed!" Without even thinking I jumped from the car, rushed to the mine phone at the power center and called outside to the dispatcher whose station was in the communication center located in the Scotia bath house. I told him we needed an ambulance on the outside and some help on our section, even though I didn't know at the time what had happened.

I rushed back to #2 heading and observed several of our mining crew struggling with a large slab of draw rock. I rushed to help lift it off our obviously badly injured co-worker. The rock was about 4ft wide, 8 ft. long and 6in. thick and almost completely covered the man. We finally managed to lift the rock off him after some difficulty. He was breathing but wasn't able to speak to us or acknowledge us.

By the time we managed to remove the large rock someone had retrieved a stretcher from the power center and we quickly loaded our buddy onto the stretcher and headed to the end of the track where a personnel track "bus" was waiting to take the injured man outside. We feared that he wouldn't be able to survive the injury he had suffered but he was a tough man and he made it to a major trauma center where he fought the fight but succumbed to his injuries a couple of days later.

The buddy and good friend we lost that night was one of the nicest people you could ever meet and he and I had worked a double shift together many times before his accidental death. Miners everywhere feel a kinship to their fellow miners and when one loses his life while working underground it affects co-workers the way it does soldiers in wartime. You feel as if you have lost one of your own family and the hurt is devastating.

It troubled me, especially since I was the last one to speak to him before his accident and knowing that it could have easily have been me instead of him. I set that jack for him and he set his 6 ft. jack ahead of the one I set. The one he set just happened to loosen a piece of slate with a crack in it which fell on him.

A few days later our whole section crew and our former section boss, Johnny Breeding, was standing beside the deceased man's family at his graveside while the preacher said a few words. Afterwards Johnny and I talked for a few minutes before we left the cemetery. Johnny and I were both Marines who had served during the Vietnam War and we felt a deep kinship because of that commonality.

I'll never forget what Johnny said to me, "Eddie, this is so sad for us all but we'll never know who'll be next, do we?" I agreed with him and we left that beautiful cemetery not knowing that just a few days later my humble friend and Marine buddy Johnny Breeding would be the next coal miner at Scotia to die.

He was relieving the continuous miner helper out at dinner time and a large slab of coal rib rolled over on him, ending his young life. He had managed to survive the Vietnam War and the absolute hellhole known as the Siege of Khe Sanh, but he couldn't survive the dangers of the subterranean depths of the Imboden coal seam beneath Big Black Mountain.

CHAPTER TEN

When the year of 1975 came to a close a total of 237 safety violations and closure orders had been issued to Scotia Coal Company by the U.S. Mine Safety and Enforcement Administration. That number included 23 total closure orders issued, nine of which were (104a) imminent danger closure orders.

From the year of 1970 through 1975, 855 notices for (Federal) health and safety violations had been issued against the company. During that same period of time the Scotia mine had been ordered closed 110 times, 39 of the closures were for imminent danger conditions.

On at least seven separate occasions between January 1974 and February 1976 MESA issued violation notices of high methane concentrations in the Scotia #1 mine. On at least two separate occasions, November 18, 1974 and January 7, 1975 the Scotia mine was ordered closed because high levels of methane were found by the MESA inspector. The January 7, 1975 closure order indicated that an imminent danger condition existed due to a combination of 1.2 percent methane and inadequate ventilation.

The explosive range of methane is between 5% and 15%, while 10% of methane present in the air is required for maximum explosive violence. The approximate ignition temperature of methane is 1200 degrees Fahrenheit. If oxygen levels are below 12% no explosion of a methane air mixture can occur. If coal dust is present when a methane explosion occurs the force of the explosion is greater. It is also possible to have an explosion when less than 5% of methane is present if coal dust is present in the air.

Good ventilation and plenty of rock dust is the key to helping prevent explosions in a "gassy" mine such as Scotia was. Mine operators, including Scotia, were required to apply rock dust in underground bituminous coal mines to reduce the explosion potential of coal dust and other dust generated during mining operations. Rock dust applied to the top, floor, and sides of all underground areas is necessary to protect miners from the potential of a coal dust explosion, or if one does occur, to reduce the severity of the explosion.

Scotia miners were aware of the role rock dusting and good ventilation practices played in the safety of their workplace and I never heard even one of them complain about having to rock dust their work areas with many bags of heavy rock dust. Neither did I ever hear

Scotia management complaining of the cost involved in having tons of rock dust available at all four Scotia mines any time it was needed.

However, there was one type of rock dust that roof bolter operators and helpers especially hated. That was the dust generated when drilling the mine roof to install resin bolts after a cut of coal was taken from the heading. That dust was the type that causes the dreaded pneumoconiosis disease that most miners fight after years of mining. While the rock dust used for covering the floor, top, and sides of the mine also contained the deadly silica, the percentage used in that type dust was 4% tops, while the rock dust in the bolter's dust box had an untold percentage and therefore possibly more deadly and harmful to the lungs and whole respiratory system.

The dust had to be cleaned out of the dust collecting box after each cut of coal was bolted with resin bolts. Raking the dust out of the box was accompanied by much coughing and trying to bring up the gobs of dust particles clinging to your throat and lungs. Even though I always wore a dust mask every possible moment when underground, my stint of almost five years as a bolt machine operator and helper had to have had a negative effect on my health. As a matter of fact I attribute my years of coal mining to having to have quadruple bypass surgery in 2016.

My heart surgeon questioned me about my diet when I was diagnosed with four blocked arteries and was flabbergasted when I told him I had been a vegetarian who had not eaten meat for the past 48 years, nor had I ever smoked. I told him about my years in the coal mines and how I had absorbed gads of rock and coal dust and other chemicals related to mining at that time. We also had to apply a porous material from five gallon buckets (with a danger warning posted on the side of the bucket) on the seals we had to build as we advanced to recover the bodies after the second explosion at the Scotia #1 mine. I'll always believe that my heart surgery was brought on (at least partly) due to my coal mining days.

In the evening of January 1976 my fellow motor operator and I took two supply car loads of supplies to a couple of coal producing sections inside New Taggart. As per the law we coupled a locomotive at each end for safety reasons. My co-worker nearly always operated the smaller 5 ton motor while I operated the 6 ton larger motor, not for any particular reason, but partially due to the fact that I was the operator of the bigger motor when I was the only motorman on the second shift when track was first laid inside the mine. The smaller motor came to New Taggart several months later. My co-worker was transferred to our mine at about the same time period.

As we approached the hill where we had come uncoupled from the supply cars a few days before, the front motor and fully loaded supply car wrecked, with both the motor and supply car having all four trucks off the track.

The wreck happened in the worst spot possible because the track there was blocked up higher than the bottom due to the awkward angle of the bottom of the mine floor. Our wreck had the track into and out of the mine completely blocked with no idea how we were going to get our equipment back on the track.

My motor was coupled to the rear car and both the supply car and my motor was still on the rails, so we uncoupled them from our wrecked vehicles and I backed the supply car and my motor off the hill out of the way. We first had to use our 5 ton railroad jacks to scoot the loaded supply car, then the locomotive from the inclined hill to a point near the track where we could jack the vehicles high enough to get above the track, then used another jack to scoot them onto the rails one truck at a time.

This took several hours to accomplish and when we finally got both wrecks back on the track we had to use blocks of wood under the leaning rails to shore them up so as to withstand the weight and frequency of traffic on them. We finally got back "on the road" and delivered our supplies after nearly 4 hours of labor. This was by far the most difficult wreck I to contend with had while working as a motorman.

After we delivered our two car loads of supplies to the two sections we headed outside into the cold night air only to have a message waiting for me that I was needed at home because my maternal grandmother had passed away in the hospital. She was 85 years old and had suffered a stroke a few days before. She had been admitted into the ICU unit of the hospital in the Whitesburg Appalachian Regional Hospital after the stroke and had been unconscious ever since.

She and I had been really close and her death came as a shock even though the family had realized she would probably not recover from the stroke. I had thought that I had trouble when our motors caused so much work on us that night, not knowing that I had lost my favorite grandmother at the very same time we were struggling to put our wreck back on the track.

Meanwhile in January and February 1976, MESA conducted an eight week inspection of the Scotia #1 mine. Also in the month of February, mining in the 2

Southeast Mains section of the Scotia #1 mine was discontinued because the height of the coal had gotten so high that the continuous miner couldn't reach the top of the coal and draw rock. The mining equipment was then moved back from the face of 2 SEM to a point about 1,800 ft. from the 2 SEM section and mining was then begun in the new section that would be known as the 2 Left Panel off Southeast Mains. The distance from the 2 Left Panel to the main line switch at the mouth of 2 southeast was 2,000 feet. A new continuous miner that could reach the high coal in 2 SEM was put on order so that section could eventually start producing coal again.

On March 8, 1976, Cecil Davis, who was a MESA Coal Mine Health Technical Specialist (Inspector) who worked out of the Whitesburg, Kentucky office of MESA, arrived at the Scotia complex to inspect the new 2 Left Panel off 2 Southeast Mains. After concluding his inspection Davis issued four notices of violations, two of which were ventilation problems. He did not inspect the 2 SEM section which was at this point idled because of the moving of the equipment of that section to start 2 Left Panel.

Normally when a new section was started, an overcast [9] was constructed in order to ventilate the new

[9] An enclosed airway constructed to provide a means for one air current to cross another.

section with the correct amount of fresh air needed for mining coal. In order to start producing coal some of the air going towards 2 SEM was diverted to the new section by means of stretching brattice cloth across the entries, which forced some of the air towards the new 2 Left Panel. Bratticemen were working on building the needed overcast by March 8 but the work had not been completed. The 2 Left Panel section had by that date driven the new section 600 foot (4 & ½ breaks) into the mountain.

By the date of March 8, 1976 Scotia employed 539 men and women at their four mine openings, 314 at their Scotia Mine #1 and a total of 225 at their other three mines, New Taggart, Upper Taggart, and the B Seam. The Scotia #1 mine was the largest of the three, producing about 2, 500 tons of coal daily.

The parent company of Scotia Coal Company was the Blue Diamond Coal Company Inc. of Knoxville, Tennessee. Blue Diamond was at the time the selling agent for the company's six coal brands, _Leatherwood, Blue Diamond, Royal Scott, Starfire, Mayflower, and Tennessee Group._

Blue Diamond had an older and larger mining operation (the Leatherwood Mine) located at Leatherwood, Perry County, Kentucky. Blue Diamond Coal Co. recognized the Southern Labor Union as its bargaining agent at the Leatherwood mine, while the Scotia Employees Association represented the employees of their Scotia mines. These two largest mining operations of Blue Diamond and a couple of smaller operations produced about 2.8 million tons of coal a year in Kentucky.

At 7:00 p.m. Monday evening on March 8, 1976, Federal Mine Inspector Cecil Davis was on the 2 Left Panel off 2 Southeast Mains conducting a routine inspection of the new section. He issued the section a total of four violations, two of which were corrected within 10 minutes of his order. One of those corrected violations was because the face brattice cloth was only maintained within 25 feet of the face instead of the 10 feet the law required. Davis directed that the violations be corrected by 4:00 p.m. the following day, March 9, 1976. It wouldn't matter now but no one knew it that evening.

CHAPTER ELEVEN

March 9th, 1976

A t 7:00 a.m. this morning the day shift crews of Scotia's #1 (bottom mine) climbed aboard their track buses and proceeded slowly down the steep New Airway entry. The six active coal producing sections together with the belt men, brattice men, belt head men, etc. numbered 106 miners headed into the Scotia mine that morning.

The temperature was cold (the low 30's) and cloudy conditions prevailed. None of them knew that only 91 of the 106 would still be alive by noon of this day.

After all the mantrips had entered the mine at around 7:30 a.m., J.P. Feltner, the Underground Construction Foreman, called Richard Combs, General Mine Foreman, and told him that he would have a load of steel rails delivered from the 1 Right off 2 East section to 2 Southeast Main section.

The plan was to deliver the rails so the track in 2 Southeast Main section could have the track extended and the section could be activated when the continuous miner that had been ordered was delivered.

After calling Mine Foreman Combs, Feltner proceeded first to the 2 Left Panel section to search for a rail bender and acetylene-oxygen tanks. After leaving 2 Left Panel, Feltner met the motor crew at the mouth of Northeast Mains where they had stopped to charge the #6 locomotive, the batteries on that motor being low on battery charge. The #6 locomotive was a 7 ton Goodman which was equipped with an air compressor as a part of the pneumatic breaking system. This compressor would "kick on" occasionally to build pressure for the brake system. Roy McKnight was the operator of #6 that morning.

The other locomotive, an 8 ton Westinghouse, was equipped with a conventional mechanical braking system and was operated that day by Lawrence Peavey. His locomotive was coupled to the load of rails and McKnight's #6 locomotive was coupled behind Peavey's.

Both locomotives weren't operating at peak capacity because the #6 had a discharged set of batteries and the #8 had only one set of trucks (wheels) working. This was not the best situation to be in because there was a very steep hill in the track entry of 2 Southeast Main that required a "run and go" to climb the hill successfully and the load of rails they were pushing weighted several tons. They would be pushing at least 8 to 10 tons of steel rails up that hill.

At 11:35, with both locomotives pushing the load of steel in front of them, they left the Northeast switch and headed toward the 2 Southeast section, about a 10 minute trip. According to later testimony they had no methane monitor with them to make any test or examination of the 2 Southeast Mains before entering the area.

Feltner left the Northeast Mains mouth for 2 Southeast Mains at the same time as the motor crew to check on his crew that were setting timbers along the track haulage road 800 feet inby the Southeast Main belt drive. A few minutes after arriving there at 11.45 a.m. he felt a gust of air moving outby, which was opposite to the normal ventilation's movement. After Feltner had confirmed that an explosion had in fact occurred he contacted all the active sections by mine phone except the 2 Left Panel off 2 Southeast Mains.

Just before the explosion roared out of the 2 Southeast Mains section and on past 2 Left Panel to the 2 Southeast Mains / Northeast Mains switch, Virgil Coots, the 2 Left Panel section foreman, talked to James Bentley, the assistant mine foreman, about losing his air on the section. Two or three minutes after talking with Bentley and telling him he was going to walk the 600 feet to the mouth of the section to check on his air, the terrible explosion occurred.

The blast killed the four men who were at the mouth of 2 Left Panel, including Coots, the foreman who had just got off the phone with James Bentley, the two men building the overcast, and the belthead man. Three other men on the 2 Left Panel were also killed by the explosion. All three were found just a few feet apart in the #4 entry of 2 Left Panel. Two others also killed instantly were the two motormen who had pushed the rails up the steep hill with their two locomotives. The total was nine miners dead from the terrible explosion's deadly blast.

Six men other men working at the face of 2 Left survived the explosion and decided to put their self-rescuers[10] on as they tried to walk out of the area, only to apparently change their minds when they reached the mouth of the section and saw the death and destruction there. The beltline and belt structure was all twisted and torn, all the surrounding coal, ribs, roof, and the passage ways were blackened and charred. The smoke likely obscured the ability to see even a few feet in front of them. For whatever reason, they decided to go back on the section and barricade.

Their barricade was constructed by using yellow brattice cloth, blocks of coal, drawrock and other loose

---

[10] Self-rescuers are good for one hour in carbon monoxide atmospheres, they do not supply oxygen.

materials to barricade an area about 20' x 20' in size. When the fresh air was exhausted behind the barricade, the six men behind it perished. Thus, a total of 15 men died inside Big Black Mountain that fateful morning.

John Hackworth was watching the 2 Southeast Mains belthead which was located nearly 3.800 feet from the point where the explosion originated. Even at that distance the force of the explosion rolled him a short distance across the mine floor. He wasn't badly injured and immediately called outside the mine to inform the dispatcher of what had happened.

He then donned his self-rescuer and traveled up the 2 Southeast track entry, but turned back after walking over 2,000 feet when the smoke got too thick to see anything.

At 12: 26 p.m., Scotia company representatives called MESA'S Whitesburg Field Office to report that the Scotia #1 mine had had an explosion in the vicinity of 2 Southeast Mains and there were 15 men unaccounted for. Inspectors from the Pikeville and Whitesburg offices of MESA were immediately dispatched to the Scotia mine.

At 1:00 p.m., the Pikeville office of MESA called the national office of MESA in Arlington, Virginia to report the sad event. Mesa's Mine Emergency Operations

Group (MEO) then arranged for an Air Force airlift of MESA'S Mine Rescue Teams and other mine rescue equipment. In the following days MEO personnel would install 10,000 feet of gas sampling tubes bundles which were connected to continuous gas analysis equipment. They also conducted a down-hole television survey at the face area of 2 Southeast Mains heading, the possible area of the explosion.

Shortly after 1:00 p.m., MESA inspectors arrived at the mine and immediately issued a 103.(f) order, an order providing that a Federal Inspector may issue a withdrawal order following a mine accident to insure the safety of any person in the mine.

Between 2:00 p.m. and 3:00 p.m., Scotia personnel tried to make a rescue attempt for the missing miners but without success. Soon after, Monroe West of the Norton, Virginia MESA office, and Bill Clemons of the Pikeville, Kentucky office of MESA arrived on scene at Scotia. A short time after, Charles Sample of the Harlan Kentucky MESA office joined them.

West and Sample then went underground to direct rescue operations, while Inspector Clemons took charge of surface operations just as the first Mine Rescue teams began arriving. Seven rescue teams from various coal companies would eventually arrive at Scotia to help in rescue efforts, although a couple of them wouldn't arrive until after eleven o'clock that evening.

By 4:00 p.m. some of the rescue teams had completed their preparations and left the surface from the office portal at 4:30 p.m., followed five minutes later by the second team. Eventually seven teams would enter the mine, all of whom were wearing their breathing apparatus. The Bethlehem Mine Rescue team stayed behind as a backup. By 5:00 p.m. the teams had established their first fresh base at the mouth of Northeast Mains and 2 Southeast Main.

Around 4:00 p.m. family members of the missing men began gathering at the Scotia entrance to wait and pray that their loved ones would be found safe and uninjured. Immediate family members were invited to await rescue efforts at the company bathhouse located near the #1 Scotia mine entrance.

The bathhouse and surrounding property were a bee hive of activity while the wait went on, with many Scotia miners also gathered on the property and in the bathhouse, hoping for the best outcome possible. It was not to be though.

The Westmoreland Mine Rescue Team found the first body of one of the missing men at 10:18 p.m. located just inby the 2 Left Panel belt drive. Nearby they located three more bodies. Then, proceeding on another 600 feet to the section face, they found behind the yellow curtained barricade the bodies of six more men.

That left only two men still missing. The National Mines Rescue Team advanced slowly towards the 2 Southeast Mains heading. Finally the two locomotives with the load of railroad steel were sighted at the end of the track and both motormen were lying dead just a few feet from their locomotives. The 15 men were now all accounted for.

After finding all the bodies, readings mine of the atmosphere were taken at the face of 2 Southeast Mains which showed a reading of 15% oxygen and 5% of methane present. Carbon Monoxide was detected also. The rescue mission of earlier in the evening was now a recovery mission.

Turning off Route 119 and across the little concrete bridge spanning the Poor Fork branch of the Cumberland River, I could see in the distance that the security guard was standing outside the Scotia guard shack. This was unusual for him, as he usually just stood in the door and waved me on through but as I approached the little shack he held his hand up for me to stop.

I rolled the window down and with a worried look he said, "I don't think there's going to be any work today, somethin' just happened in the bottom (#1) mine." "What happened," I asked. "Don't know for sure but they think we might have had an explosion down there and I believe some of the miners are still missing because they haven't heard from one section yet. You can go on in if you want to, they might need some help. Anyway, they didn't say to stop any employees from coming in."

After our conversation I drove on to the bath house which was a quarter mile from the guard shack. As I pulled in the parking lot I noticed a rail bus that had just came up the slope with a crew of miners inside. I didn't know it then but all the mine sections had been called out of the mine when management had heard from the 2 Southeast beltman who had called outside with the news of an explosion on 2 Left.

As I walked into the bathhouse I noticed a lot of the day shift were already out of the mine and were in the showers. A few were already showered and dressed and were just sitting on the benches discussing what little they knew about the explosions, Some said they felt the air change around the time of the explosion while others said they heard and felt nothing and knew little or nothing about what had happened.

Some of the New Taggart crew began to come into the bathhouse a few minutes after I arrived and as they did we sat on the wooden benches and tried to come to terms with what might have just happened in the bottom mine. I believe nearly all of us sitting there that day thought that eventually all the men would successfully emerge up the slope entry and go home to their families, although rumors were swirling all around the bathhouse that some or all of the 2 Left Panel crew might have perished since they hadn't been heard from yet.

Most day shift crew stayed around the bathhouse and the communications room located there. They were hoping to hear good news before they went home but eventually some decided to go home and await developments there. I was one of those that decided to stay around to try to find out exactly what was going on.

My brother Jimmy, who worked on the same shift and at the same mine as I did,stayed for a few hours, then decided to go home to assure the family he and I were O.K. It's fortunate that he left when he did because our family members were among those who were gathered at the Scotia mine entrance at the Poor Fork bridge, waiting to see if we were among the missing.

They didn't know we had arrived at the mine after the explosion and hadn't even been inside the New Taggart mine that day. Nor did they know which mine the missing men were missing from. For some reason I didn't even think about calling home to let them know I was alright. What was worse was that my wife and children had heard about the possible explosion at the Scotia mine and had no way to get there because my wife hadn't yet learned to drive.

My dad, mom, and sister Kathy had gathered near the bridge that afternoon and they recognized Jimmy's Volkswagen coming out of the Scotia complex and only then was my mom convinced that at least one of us was safe. After Jimmy stopped and told them that I was safe also, did they breathe a sigh of relief. Many of those family members of those still trapped were gathered there at the bridge and the news they received later that night would change their lives forever.

Late that evening, (around 4:00 p.m.) a company representative went to the bridge near the guard shack where a large crowd of news people and family members had gathered to await news of the missing miners. He invited family members gathered there to come to the Scotia bathhouse where it was warm and the Scotia communications center was located. This was where the dispatcher of Scotia rail traffic and communications inside the Scotia mine's working sections was routinely monitored. This evening it would be the focal point for those waiting for word of their loved ones.

At 10:15 p.m., the first body was found by the Westmoreland Mine Rescue Team. Those of us sitting around the bathhouse, including Scotia miners, company officials, and some family members, heard the terrible news as it filtered from the dispatcher's crowded office.

The first missing miner had been found. It crushed the hopes all of those of us waiting around hoping for good news but receiving the news everyone had been dreading. One or two people came out of the dispatcher's office sobbing and the rest of us just sit there inside the bathhouse stunned with the news. Those missing men were our friends, co-workers, and neighbors. We had all been praying for their safe return from the depths of Black Mountain but it was not to be.

CHAPTER TWELVE

Chronology of First Explosion[11]

*J*anuary-February 1976: MESA conducted an 8-week inspection of entire Scotia mine.
February 1976 – Mining in 2 Southeast main (2 SEM) section was discontinued due to the height of the coal seam and lack of equipment. Mining machinery was moved back from the face of 2 SEM and mining was begun in the 2 Left Panel, off 2 SEM.

March 1976 – Scotia submitted to MESA a proposed new ventilation plan for the mine.

March 8, 1976, 2nd shift – MESA Coal Mine Health Technical Specialist Cecil Davis, stationed at Whitesburg, Kentucky made an inspection of the 2 Left Panel, off 2 SEM. Davis issued 4 notices of violations, 2 of which were for ventilation problems. Davis did not inspect 2 SEM.

March 8-9, 1976 3rd shift –Scotia fire boss Charles Fields conducted a preshift examination of Scotia Mine but failed to inspect 2 SEM.

---

[11] Scotia Coal Mine Disaster, March 9, 1976 A Staff Report

March 9, 1976 – During the morning, two miners were sent into 2 SEM to take steel rails into the section for storage. Two locomotives were used to push steel loaded cars into the area.

11:00 a.m. – James Bentley, Assistant Mine Foreman in charge of ventilation, noticed a regulator governing air intake had been left open, thereby changing ventilation patterns in the mine, Bentley closed the regulator.

11:15 a.m. – Bentley called the mine foreman and asked for a ventilation check. Bentley then called Virgil Coots, foreman on 2 Left Panel off 2SEM and asked for an air reading. Coots said he "just lost" his ventilation. Bentley told him to check his curtains and call him back. Time about 11:30 a.m.

11:35 a.m. – First explosion occurred in 2 SEM.

12:26 p.m. – Scotia reported accident to MESA.'s Whitesburg, Kentucky office as an ignition.

12:45 p.m. – Scotia informed MESA of an explosion with 15 men unaccounted for; MESA Inspectors were dispatched.

12:50 p.m. – MESA Pikeville office notified MESA.'s national office in Arlington, Virginia of the accident.

1:10 p.m. – MESA inspectors at mine issued a 103(f) order, effectively controlling entry into Scotia mine.

3:00 p.m. – Scotia personnel attempted rescue efforts but failed to make any progress.

3:00 p.m. – First mine rescue teams arrived; other teams continued to arrive until 11:00 p.m. that evening.

3:15 p.m. – MESA. officials Monroe West, Sub district Manager, Norton, Virginia office and William Clemons, Assistant District Manager Pikeville, Kentucky office arrived at the mine. Charles Sample, MESA. Coal Mine Inspection Supervisor, Harlan, Kentucky arrived soon after. West and Sample went underground to direct rescue operations; Clemons took charge on the surface.

4:30 p.m. – First mine rescue team went underground.

4:35 p.m. – Second mine rescue team went underground.

6:55 p.m. – Fresh air base established.

8:30 p.m. – MESA. Administrator Robert Barrett, Assistant Administrator John Crawford, and R. Peluso Assistant Administrator Technical Support, arrived at the mine, after briefing, all three went underground.

10:00 p.m. – Barrett and company arrived at the fresh air base and began assisting in the operations.

10:15 p.m. – First body was found in area of 2 SEM by the Westmoreland Coal Company rescue team.

As if the death of the fifteen Scotia miners hadn't been enough tragedy for one day, a Harlan County man whose son-in-law was reportedly trapped in the Scotia mine was killed in an automobile accident while rushing along with members of his family to the Scotia mine.

The twenty one year old man driving the other automobile was taken to the Letcher County Jail and was charged with second degree manslaughter and later released on $10,000 bond. The accident occurred approximately two miles from the Scotia mine.[12]

In another incident related to the explosion at Scotia, a Cumberland, Kentucky man was arrested for shooting at the Cumberland police chief who was en route to the scene of the Scotia mine explosion. Authorities arrested the 37 year old suspect and charged him with two counts of wanton endangerment. The police chief stated that the suspect had knocked out the headlights of his car. The town of Cumberland is located about 14 miles from the Scotia mine.

---

[12] Letcher County Community Press

After the first body had been found and the information had been related to the authorities who were waiting outside the mine, those of us still sitting around the bathhouse fell into a somber mood. Speaking was done in whispers and much reflection of the day's events was being discussed by the few assembled miners who were still waiting there. We realized for the first time that more bad news would soon follow, as all the men of the section worked in the same area.

By the time of the midnight hour we had gotten affirmation that more bodies had been found. Any hope that some of the men would be found alive was fading quickly by that time.

CHAPTER THIRTEEN

March 10, 1976

By 1: 30 a.m. all the bodies had been located and the process of transporting them to the outside was put into action. Three steel rail supply cars were backed into the shop section of the supply house which had facilities for repairing rail vehicles. In that large building, bright yellow brattice cloth was carefully spread over the supply cars' bottoms in preparation to send inside the cars inside to transport the bodies to the Scotia mine entrance.

A little after 1:30 a.m. two locomotives, one coupled to the front of the supply cars, the other to the back, proceeded slowly down the slope track entry which was located just behind the bathhouse. Several miners (including myself) were standing on the bridge which spanned the deep cut of the slope. The bridge was used for a shortcut to the upper Scotia parking lot. From there we would have the best view of the slope portal when the miners were brought out of the mine.

At 2:00 a.m. The motor crew arrived at the fresh air base which was established about 1,000 feet from the

2 Left Panel section and approximately 1,800 feet from the 2 Southeast section. All fifteen bodies would have to be carried to the end of the track at the fresh air base, 13 of them from the 2 Left Panel and two of them from the head of 2 Southeast section near the locomotives they had pushed the rails into that section with that morning.

Around 3:30 a.m. the bodies had been carefully and respectfully loaded into the three supply cars and the yellow brattice cloth spread across the cars and fastened to the sides. The locomotives and supply cars then proceeded down the 2 Southeast Mains track the 4 & ½ or 5 miles to the steep slope entry with their precious cargo under the yellow brattice cloth.

We miners who were still there that morning had followed the motors and supply cars progress from the mine by checking with the dispatcher located in the bathhouse and we were standing on the bridge at 4:46 a.m. when the first locomotive emerged from the mouth of the slope entrance. The three yellow cloth draped supply cars were coupled to the front motor and the other locomotive was coupled to the back of the cars.

Even though it was still dark at that hour the lights from the bathhouse was sufficient to clearly make out the still forms under the yellow brattice cloth. No one spoke as the train proceeded up the slope very slowly.

Each of us had our own subdued thoughts just then and preferred the silence except for the sound of the battery motors as they traveled up the track and around the steep curve at the top of the hill, then to the company maintenance shop, the temporary morgue.

After unhooking one of the locomotives, the other backed the two supply cars into the shop building and the doors were closed. The medical personnel, funeral directors, and coroners were now with the bodies and at least 15 ambulances were scattered in the Scotia complex, waiting to pick up the deceased miners. They had been gathering since the first body was found and it was a strain on some of the local funeral homes to have enough suitable vehicles to transport the bodies of the miners, most of whom were from Harlan County, Kentucky. Only four of the deceased men were from Letcher County, where the Scotia mine was located.

Those that were there as reporters for newspapers and other media outlets were required to wait at the outside entrance to Scotia, which was located about ½ mile from the Scotia main office complex. Most would stay there until the news of the finding of the deceased miners began filtering out to the bridge area where many relatives were also waiting.

At some point MESA Chief Robert Barrett flew in from Washington D.C. and immediately went into the #1 mine to access the situation for himself. Some others arriving on site at Scotia was U.S. Representative Tim Lee Carter and Representative Carl D. Perkins who was the congressman that represented Kentucky's Congressional District seven which included Letcher County and Oven Fork. H.N. Kirkpatrick, Commissioner of the Kentucky Department of Mines and Minerals was also at the mine.

The names of the deceased miners weren't released immediately. It would be nearly 12 hours before the names were released to the public.

Names of the fifteen men killed in the first mine explosion at Scotia on March 9, 1976.

Name	Classification	Age
Dennis Boggs	Utility Man	27
Everett S. Combs	Ventilation	29
Virgil Coots	Section Foreman	24
Earl Galloway	Shuttle Car Opr.	44
David Gibbs	Repairman	30
Robert Griffith	Belt Cleaner	24
Larry D. McKnight	Motorman	28
Roy McKnight	Timberman	31
Lawrence Peavy	Supplyman	25
Tommy R. Scott	Miner Opr.	24
Ivan G. Sparkman	Bratticeman	34
Jimmy W. Sturgill	Utility Man	20
Kenneth Turner	Roof Bolter	25
Willie D. Turner	Shuttle Car Opr.	25
Denver Widner	Ventilation	31

At 5:00 a.m. on March 10, 1976 after the bodies were out of the mine and had been turned over to the families and funeral directors MESA officials met to consider how to move forward with the investigation of the explosion's cause. It was decided at this meeting that MESA rescue teams, and Scotia personnel would enter the mine on the second shift on March 11 to try to reestablish ventilation to the mine. It was also agreed to reenter the mine the next day, March 11, to conduct an inspection tour.

The next day, March 10, at 4:00 p.m., two teams of MESA Inspectors, Company officials, and Scotia Employees Union Representatives entered the Imboden mine from the slope portal and began exploring toward the area of the explosion.

When they reached the 2 Southeast Mains switch, they discovered that a sagging and overhanging rock would have to be bolted before they could get supplies via track motors to restore the ventilation in the 2 Left Panel and 2 Southeast heading. To do this a roof bolting machine would have to be brought from the nearby Northeast Main area and using the power center located at the 2 Southeast to supply power to the bolter. The overhanging rock to be bolted was located from 300 to

500 feet from the power center and the 2 Southeast Mains switch.

MESA and Company officials slowly advanced to the last fresh air base established a few hours earlier by the rescue teams when recovering the bodies. This was located at the 2 Left and 2 Southeast Mains intersection. No attempt was made to go any further because of the low oxygen (12%) and high methane (5%) reading taken at the time the bodies were removed from the area.

At 12:48 a.m. March 11, MESA Inspectors and Company officials returned to the surface and discussed the need for the loose rock to be bolted at the mouth of 2 Southeast Mains. Another meeting was held at 2:05 a.m. to discuss ventilation plans with a MESA ventilation expert and to prepare a set of recommendations of how to move forward with those plans.

Meanwhile, after watching the deceased miners being transported from the mine I left the Scotia mine property and finally arrived at my home in Colson, Kentucky after over 20 hours spent in the mine bathhouse without sleep. I slept very little that morning after returning home and was up before noon.

Having been told before leaving Scotia property that there would be no work for Scotia employees at the three upper mines for the next two days, I was surprised when my wife answered the phone on the morning of March 11 and said the Scotia secretary wanted to speak to me.

She informed me that a crew of men was entering the #1 Scotia mine later that evening to bolt a rock near the explosion site so the mine could be further explored. She said they needed a motorman to help transport the men and equipment needed for the job. I was again surprised because I had never worked in the bottom mine but had spent most of my time at the New Taggart mine where the conditions were very different from the #1 bottom mine. At that time I had never even been inside the #1 mine, but had heard many rumors concerning the dangerous roof conditions and methane problems encountered there.

When my wife heard my conservation with the secretary and while I was still on the phone she spoke loudly, "You're not going to work in that mine!" I glanced at her and shook my head as if to tell her to be quiet, but she then said, "You've got children here that want you to stay home!"

The lady on the phone then said to me, "That's alright, your wife is concerned and doesn't want you to work, so I'll call someone else to help, it's all voluntary work anyway. I was embarrassed by the fact that the secretary had heard my wife's concern with my being called to work so soon after the explosion.

After hanging up, Wanda and I had this discussion: She: "You know that mine could easily blow up again, why even think about working down there?" In my own moment of misguided wisdom, I replied, "You're just over reacting, there's no way they would ask us to go into that mine if there was any danger of another explosion. All you've done is cause me to lose a shift of work!"

That night a little after midnight, I was lying in bed and listening to a Chicago radio station when I heard these words from the announcer, "There has been another explosion in the Scotia coal mine located in Oven Fork, Kentucky!

Chronology March 10, 1976

1:20 a.m. – All 15 bodies were located and removed. Five bodies were located in main shaft of 2 SEM at the intersection of 2 Left Panel, and eight bodies were discovered behind a makeshift curtain barricade in the 2 Left Panel. Two bodies were discovered by National Mine Rescue team farther up 2 SEM towards the face near the two locomotives. The mine area in the vicinity of the locomotives was described as showing the most damage.

4:46 a.m. – The bodies arrived at the surface. All personnel were withdrawn from the mine.

Early morning hours – A meeting of MESA, state, company officials and miners was held to decide future actions. It was decided that MESA rescue teams and Scotia personnel would work during the 2nd shift to restore ventilation to mine. It was also agreed to reenter mine for an inspection tour beginning at 7:00 a.m. on 3-11-76. After this meeting, MESA Washington personnel departed.

7:30-8:00 a.m. – William Clemons went home; Russell Tackett of MESA was left in charge. Clemons returned to mine later in the day, prior to 2nd shift, and resumed control.

5:00 p.m. – At the suggestion of Ben Taylor, MESA Coal Mine Inspection Supervisor, Whitesburg, Kentucky, Taylor and Richard Combs, Scotia General Mine Foreman, began to pre-shift inspect part of mine, (not up to SEM). Taylor was told by Combs of a compressor on a locomotive near face of 2 SEM. Taylor asked Combs if a locomotive-compressor could have been a possible ignition source. Taylor did not immediately report this conversation to other officials.

6:55 p.m. – Two MESA teams entered the mine to reestablish ventilation and explore 2 SEM. They discovered a hazardous roof condition. They also determined that ventilation would be difficult to restore. They prepared to return to the surface to make their report of the roof and ventilation conditions they had encountered.

CHAPTER FOURTEEN

March 11, 1976

Early in the morning of March 11, MESA and Scotia employees inspected the Scotia mine for hazardous conditions except for the 2 SEM section where ventilation hadn't been restored.

Inspector Clemons returned to the mine around 3:00 p.m. where the Scotia employees that had volunteered to go into the mine to bolt the rock at 2 SEM switch were assembling to go into the mine. At 4:00 p.m. ten company employees and three Federal Inspectors went underground. Two of the Scotia employees would take two locomotives and two supply cars inside the mine with them.

One of the Scotia employees who would accompany the crew was J.B. Holbrook, who was the Secretary of the Scotia Employees association, the union that represented the hourly employees of Scotia. He was a classified tipple operator and never been inside the Scotia mine before. James Williams was also going inside with the crew, as he was the 2nd shift foreman of 2 Left Panel section.

The other crew members were Scotia employees Don Creech, Earnest Collins, Don Polly, Rick Parker, Glen Barker, Monroe Sturgill James Sturgill, and John Hackworth. Hackworth was tending the Northeast Mains head drive when the first explosion occurred. Three MESA Federal Mine Inspectors made up the remainder of the 13 man crew going into the mine. They were Grover Tussey, Richard Sammons, and Kenneth Kiser,

Proceeding into the mine the crew traveled to Northeast Mains which was located near where the 376 foot shaft elevator was in the process of being completed when the mine exploded.

The roof bolter they intended taking from Northeast Mains to the 2 Southeast main line track switch had to have some minor repairs before being moved and by the time power had been energized and the repairs completed it was 9:30 p.m.

At 10:30 they called outside the mine to report they had reached the halfway point from their destination at Northeast Mains – 2 Southeast Mains switch. Nearly one hour later, at 11:10 p.m. they reached the switch near where the power center was located and where the roof bolter cathead would be connected to have power to bolt the dangerous rock to the mine roof.

The rock to be bolted was located only a few hundred feet from the track going into the 2 Left Panel and 2 SEM sections but it being near the end of the shift for the crew it was decided that the two repairmen would only drag the bolt machine cable to the power center just one break (about 90') away and leave the actual bolting to be done by another crew in the morning.

The two MESA Inspectors and Don Polly walked towards the rock to be bolted to check the conditions and the two repairmen had finished dragging the bolter cable around and behind the block of coal at 11:20 p.m. when a tremendous explosion roared from the 2 SEM – 2 Left Panel area and immediately killed eleven members of the 13 man crew. Eight of the men killed were gathered around the locomotives and supply car, preparing to go outside, as their shift was ending at 12:00 a.m.

Three of them were in the track entry coming out of the 2 Left – 2 SEM sections and were blown by the terrific force of the explosion several hundred feet into a brattice near the parked locomotives and supply cars. The other eight men were sitting and standing around the locomotives and two supply cars, preparing to head for the outside when the electricians finished hooking up the power to the roof bolter.

Although the eight men around the locomotives were partially hidden from the blast's deadly force, they were likely felled immediately. Only two of them were in front of the locomotives as if they heard the roar coming down the mine entries toward their location and began trying to escape the blast.

The two repairmen, (Rick Parker and Ernie Collins,) were around the block and hidden from the main force of the explosion and were trying to hook up the bolting machine cat head when the destructive force of the explosion hit the 2 SEM switch. They said later that they heard the initial explosion from the direction of the first explosion and that it took a few seconds to reach their location before the pressure and force of the blast was felt.

Parker and Collins were in the dark literally, as the black smoke and darkness of the scorched area enveloped them. They were stunned but fortunate that their injuries were minor since a gob pile near the power center had protected them from the major force of the blast. After a short time of recovery from the effects of what had just happened, Parker managed to remove his carbon monoxide self-rescuer from his mining belt and get it around his neck and mouth. Collins retrieved his self-rescuer but was unable to get the rescuer's lid off.

Parker caught up with Collins and helped Collins put it on in the smoke filled darkness.

Being well acquainted with the area, they felt their way around the block of coal and felt for the outside telephone line strung along near the top of the mine roof. Managing to take hold of the wire they felt their way along the trackway towards the outside for about a mile until they reached the Northeast-Southeast Mains junction, located 4 & 1/2 miles from the outside portal. When they reached the junction they heard a voice on the mine phone stationed there paging for someone to answer the phone. Parker answered the phone and quickly explaining their situation, he was told that they were to stay right where they were and someone would pick them up. They decided to walk on towards the outside anyway and soon met Richard Combs, General Mine Foreman of #1 Scotia mine, and Federal Inspector Davis coming to pick them up in a mine bus. At 12:30 A. M. on March 12th they reached the outside, a little over one hour after the explosion at 2Southeast Mains and 2 Left Panel.

At 1:00 a.m. MESA'S national office in Arlington, Virginia was once again notified of an explosion at the Scotia coal mine, Again MESA'S Mine Rescue Teams were ordered airlifted to the mine, and to reactivate MESA'S Mine Emergency Operations Plan.

Ambulances and police cars with sirens blaring and local officials once again were seen rushing along Route 119 to the Scotia Mine just two days after they had done so after the first explosion.

Following the explosion, two MESA officials walked into the mine via the slope portal, followed by two rescue team members. After walking over three miles to the 2 East Main intersection, they continued toward 2 East for about 800 feet where they discovered that the air flow was reversed. The four men were then withdrawn from the mine using the same route by which they had traveled into the mine.

Two rescue team members who were waiting at the bathhouse portal on the outside were sent into the mine to establish a fresh air base at the entrance to 2 East and to examine the area and the extent of any ventilation damage there. They reported an overcast at that location had been damaged and that the air was short-circuited as a result. A decision was made by MESA Inspector Clemons to withdraw the rescue teams and to concentrate all further efforts of potential rescue or recovery of the miners at 2 Southeast Mains – 2 Left Panel switch from the Frank's Creek borehole, which was then in the finishing stages of completion.

The 386 foot deep shaft of the borehole was without the elevator which was to be installed to lower miners and supplies into the further reaches of the Scotia #1 mine. The distance by road from the Scotia bathhouse portal was about six miles.

Just before 9:00 a.m. March 12, two Federal Inspectors, West and Merritt, and Scotia Employees Representative David McKnight were lowered down the borehole by means of a rope and bucket to do a pre-examination of the Northeast Main where the bottom of the shaft was located. Their inspection revealed that the ventilation was intact in that area.

After 45 minutes underground West, Merritt, and McKnight were withdrawn up the shaft and made their report to officials. In a short while Inspector Clemons, the Nos. 1 and 2 Westmoreland Coal Company Rescue Teams and the National Mines Rescue Team were lowered into the shaft. At the bottom of the shaft Clemons instructed the two Westmoreland Rescue Teams to travel along the Northeast Main track entry without using breathing apparatus, in intake air toward 2 Southeast Mains where the miners were caught in the 2nd explosion. He then assigned the National Mines Rescue Team to stay at the bottom of the shaft as a backup. The Beth-

Elkhorn Team would be on standby on the surface at the borehole entrance.

The Westmoreland teams advanced slowly towards the mouth of 2 Southeast Mains while frequently taking methane and oxygen checks as they advanced towards the area of the where the miners had been hit by the second explosion. The distance to travel was about one mile.

At around 12:00 Noon, they reached the area of the switch where they found the bodies of the eleven men who had perished there just a few hours before. The teams were then ordered back to the shaft and outside without the recovery of the bodies because of the danger of another explosion occurring. By 1:02 p.m., all the rescue teams and MESA officials were back outside the air shaft.

MESA administrator Barrett arrived back at Scotia in the early morning hours of March 12, and after meeting with mine management, the Scotia Employees Association, the Kentucky Department of Mines and Minerals, MESA, and representatives from the Department of the Interior, made the decision to seal all openings of the Scotia Mine. The mine portals were then sealed by using a double row of concrete blocks with a porous material in the middle of the blocks. After sealing, a few leaks were detected and the seals were then reinforced and the leaks were stopped.

By March 19, at 2:10 p.m., all the #1 Scotia mine entries had been sealed and the waiting began for the families of the eight Scotia miners and three MESA Inspectors. Scotia miners discussed among ourselves how long it might take before the might be reopened again, some thought it would only be a few weeks, others thought it might be a month or two, and a few even reasoned that it might never be reopened. The differences of opinion were varied and broad among the Scotia miners. In the end it would be two hundred and fifty three days.

CHRONOLOGY: March 11-12-19, 1976

March 11

12:48 a.m. – MESA teams returned to the surface and reported the roof condition and ventilation problems.

2:05 a.m. – Company, MESA, and State officials met to decide future course of action. At the meeting, it was decided to postpone a proposed inspection tour until roof repairs were made and ventilation was restored. It was decided to begin the repair work on 2nd shift, later in the day.

4:00 a.m. – William Clemons left the mine; John Smith and John Banks, two MESA. inspectors, were put in charge. Clemons returned at 2:30-3:00 p.m. and resumed control.

8:14 a.m. – MESA and Scotia employees inspected the mine for hazardous conditions except for the 2 SEM sections where ventilation had not been restored.

6:00 p.m. – Thirteen men, including three MESA. inspectors, went underground to repair the roof and restore ventilation. Since the roof bolting machine needed to be repaired and moved to 2 SEM, the team did not arrive near the entrance to 2 SEM until much later.

7:00-8:00 p.m. – Ben Taylor of MESA. returned to the mine after resting and told Clemons about the locomotive and compressor in 2 SEM. Clemons did not consider it important.

9:00 p.m. – William Clemons went home; Ben Taylor was left in charge.

11:20 p.m. – Second explosion occurred in 2 SEM. Rick Parker and Earnest Collins, the two survivors, worked their way to belt telephone and made the first call, reporting the explosion.

11.40 p.m. – News of explosion reached surface by way of the survivors' phone call. Taylor, fearing further danger, did not attempt a rescue effort. Taylor called Clemons and related the information.

March 12, 1976

12:12 a.m. – The two survivors reached good air and made 2nd phone call. Survivors were told to wait for help, but they continued.

12:20 a.m. – Rescue men were sent into the mine for survivors who were found close to the mine entrance. Rescue teams were contacted.

12:59 a.m. – William Clemons returned to the mine and resumed control. Rescue attempts were made to reach the trapped miners but because of an air reversal, the attempts were abandoned.

6:55 a.m. – Two MESA. inspectors and miner representative were lowered down an air shaft where the air was adequate.

9:45 a.m. – Three rescue teams were lowered down the shaft into mine.

12:00 Noon – Eleven bodies were found but not recovered.

1:02 p.m. – All rescue teams brought to surface.

March 19, 1976

2:10 p.m. – Mine ordered sealed.[13]

---

[13] Scotia Coal Mine Disaster: A Staff Report, Oct. 15, 1976.

CHAPTER FIFTEEN

Miners Killed In Second Explosion

Name	Classification	Age
Glenn Barker	Motorman	29
Don Creech	Utility Man	30
John Hackworth	Timberman	29
J.B. Holbrook	Tipple operator	43
Kenneth Kiser	Federal Mine Insp.	45
Carl Polly	Roof Bolter	47
Richard Sammons	Federal Mine Insp.	55
James Sturgill	Roof Bolter	40
Monroe Sturgill	Roof Bolter	40
Grover Tussey	Federal Mine Insp.	45
James Williams	Section Foreman	23

The two explosions of March 9 and 11, 1976, was a devastating blow to the Scotia employees and to Blue Diamond Coal Company, the parent company and owner of Scotia Coal Company. Some miners vowed they would never go back into a Scotia coal mine again, a few quit their jobs with the company, and on at least one occasion a Scotia miner took his own life only five days after the second explosion.

The miner was apparently deeply troubled by the deaths of the men he had worked with. His wife stated that he had not been able to "get straightened out" since the first explosion and he had worked with the 15 men who died in that explosion and was a friend of theirs.

He was scheduled to work on the midnight shift the night of the second explosion and had been "upset and depressed" since then. His wife said he had also "been hearing voices of the dead miners."[14]

One young miner who had been working for Scotia for 18 months prior to the explosions expressed his intentions this way: *"They say money isn't everything, and buddy, that's the truth. I'm going back there* (to Scotia) *just one more time, to pick up my clothes at the bathhouse."* He added, *"I went to work there for the money. That's all. They paid real good and they had that bonus for perfect attendance."*

The same miner also made comments about safety standards at Scotia: *"There's things about the mine I never liked. The air—it gets so hot I'm in a sweat after*

---

[14] Letcher County Mountain Eagle, March 25, 1976.

one cable splice. Some of the equipment's twice as old as me. But I never worked any other mine, can't really make any comparisons."

He stated that sometimes his section works a whole shift about supervision. *"I don't know where the foreman was, or even if he was in the mines. Nobody seemed to care as long as we get paid."*

Comments from other miners were just as concerning about safety standards they had observed. A miner of six years said he had observed a chronic problem with inadequate ventilation in the bottom (# 1) mine. *"There's not enough air in there,"* he said, referring to the Southeast section. *"There's never been enough air there."*

Another miner vowed, *"I'm not going back into that mine until they get an inspector in each of the five sections. That way they'll see just how much air is in there."*[15]

One Scotia coal miner who had been operating a shuttle car at the Upper Taggart mine for almost two years stated that he was instructed in the use of a self-rescuer "for the first time ever." *"Since the explosion(s) they've been cracking down on safety. But if that hadn't*

---

[15] Whitesburg Mountain Eagle March 11, 1976.

happened you can bet we wouldn't have been taught that self-rescuer."

Where ever the blame lay for the two devastating mine explosions, there was enough blame to go around. At the time of the first explosion Scotia Coal Company was in charge of the mine, while the #1 mine at the time of the second explosion, the mine was in charge of Federal MESA officials.

In the days following the twin explosions, families of the Scotia miners and Federal Inspectors who died in the explosions held their funerals and said their good-byes to their loved ones in funeral homes and local churches in the towns, hills, and hollers of Eastern Kentucky and nearby Pound, Virginia. The funerals were well attended with large crowds of people gathering, including some mourners that might not have known any of the miners.

The miners were taken to several different funeral homes in the area after their recovery from the mine:

Tri-City Funeral Home, Cumberland, Kentucky: **David Gibbs, Virgil Coots, Gail Sparkman, Kenny Turner, Denver Widner.**

Parker Funeral Home, Cumberland, Kentucky: **Roy McKnight, Larry McKnight, Everett Scottie Combs, Willie Turner.**

Colonial Chapel, Harlan, Kentucky: **Jimmy Sturgill.**

Blair Funeral Home, Whitesburg, Kentucky: **Tom Scott, Earl Galloway**

Johnson Funeral Home, Benham, Kentucky: **Lawrence Peavy.**

Banks Funeral Home, Neon, Kentucky. **Robert Griffith.**

Baker Funeral Home, Pound, Virginia. **Dennis Boggs.**

Coal miners are a close knit group because of having to work in such a dangerous environment where each individual has to watch out for his or her buddy because of those many dangers in a coal mine. This closeness resulted in lots of grief and soul searching in the coming weeks, months and years. The miners realized it could easily have been themselves that lost their lives. The possibility was very real every time a miner stepped inside a mine portal. Only good luck and watching out for yourself and your buddy could keep you from serious injury or death while underground.

After the sealing of the #1 Scotia mine, Robert Barrett, administrator of the Mining Enforcement and Safety Administration, (MESA.) stated that investigations that could lead to federal criminal charges against some of Scotia Coal Company's salaried officials were under way. According to information from MESA officials and Scotia miners (at that time) probes were being made of at least six incidents from which at least six charges could stem. They would include failure of the company to report at least one methane feeder and failure to adequately ventilate the area where the explosions occurred, both through the removal of a ventilation stopping and the hanging of curtains over fresh air passageways into the area.

Beginning in the first week of April, 1976, the Department of the Interior held two weeks of hearings in the Whitesburg, Kentucky, on the causes of the Scotia Explosions. Robert Barrett, Mine Enforcement and Safety Administrator, was appointed panel chairman. The hearings interviewed over fifty Scotia mine officials and employees during the hearings about safety issues and the extent of the miners training at Scotia. Many testified of the lack of proper training and safety measures of the mine.

One day of public hearings on the explosions were held in Washington D.C. by the Subcommittee on Labor on March 24, 1976, and three days of public hearings were conducted by a joint committee of the House Education and Labor Committee and the Senate Labor and Public Welfare Committee on May 7, May 13, and June 16, 1976, in Washington.

The last week of March, 1976, the Scotia Company sent $5,000 checks to the 26 families of the deceased coal miners. This was the result of an agreement between the company and Scotia Employees Association, the independent union representing the Scotia miners.

A memorial service was held for the deceased miners on March 21 1976, at the First Baptist Church in Whitesburg, Kentucky. Wade M. Hughes, pastor of the Lynch Church of God, and the Reverend Bill Mackey of the First Baptist church, delivered sermons in tribute to the 26 deceased miners. Letcher County Judge Estill Blair spoke at the ceremony and the First Baptist Church choir sang at the services.

In the wake of the Scotia explosions the United Mine Workers of America announced they were ready to launch an organizing drive at the company. The UMWA'S effort at organizing Scotia workers failed in 1965-1966 and the workers eventually created their own union, the Scotia Employees Association, in the early 1970's. After the UMWA'S announcement, the Justus Mine, located in McCreary County, Kentucky, voted 126 to 57 to be represented by the United Mine Workers

(UMW) Union. Like Scotia, the Justus mine was owned by Blue Diamond Coal Company at that time.

By March 19, 1976 the mine had been sealed and a meeting had been held by Company and Scotia Employees Union officials to discuss the situation surrounding the resumption of producing coal at the Scotia upper mines located on the side of Black Mountain. A meeting was held by the Company officials and the Scotia Employees to announce a temporary layoff of some Scotia workers until the #1 mine could be restored to production sometime in the future. Of course that would only happen after the bodies of the eleven men still inside the mine could be brought out of the mine.

The meeting was held in the upper Scotia parking lot located above the bathhouse in a large flat. Around 400 -450 Scotia workers were gathered around a pickup truck bed that Union and Company officials were standing in so everyone could hear and see who was speaking.

They announced that since the #1 mine wasn't able to produce coal that some workers would have to be put on a layoff panel. While Upper Taggart, B Seam, and New Taggart wasn't affected by the explosions, the layoffs would have to be by contract rules, which stipulated that layoffs would be by seniority in classification, not seniority by time at Scotia. Some murmuring was heard at the announcement, as that meant some men with more time at Scotia would probably be lain off instead of later hires.

Since I had time on a couple of other motormen I was fortunate enough to keep my job at New Taggart where I had been working for a little over 1 & ½ years. My motorman buddy also kept his job and classification at New Taggart.

Some Scotia #1 miners were scattered among the three upper mines and kept their jobs, while some of the men working at the upper mines were lain off. Approximately one half of the 526 employees were furloughed until the eventual reopening of the bottom mine.

When the three upper mines began producing coal again a few days after the #1 mine was sealed, many of the #1 mine employees reported to their new work sites. Some of them had been in the bottom mine since their hiring by Scotia and found conditions in the upper mines much different than where they had been working, especially the height of the coal.

While the bottom mine had coal height that averaged around 6 foot and higher, the upper mines had hardly any coal of that height unless a streak of drawrock was encountered and had to be mined along with the coal seam. This was what some of those who were transferred to the upper mines had been dreading. If you were an upper mine worker engaged in speaking with a #1 mine worker in the bathhouse before the explosions, he would likely have told you that, *"I hear your mine (upper mine) has low coal, I don't believe I would want to work in coal like that."* The upper mine employee would likely reply, *"I hear the bottom mine is real "gassy" and the top (roof) is falling out everywhere. I sure wouldn't want to work down there!"*

The transferred miners had some difficulty at first with the new conditions they faced at the B Seam, Upper Taggart, and New Taggart mines, but after a couple of weeks they got the soreness out of their leg and back muscles from having to walk around stooped over most of the time and became adjusted to lower roof conditions. After all, they were coal miners and miners have to learn how to adjust to changing conditions in the mine all the time. One good difference was the fact that the upper mines found no problem at all with high concentrations of methane. The fresh air was always sufficient there and very little methane, if any, was to be found when checking for methane in the coal producing face sections.

CHAPTER SIXTEEN

The fact that Scotia had no mine rescue team at the time of the explosions was addressed by management authorizing the forming of three separate rescue teams to prepare for the reopening of the bottom mine, restoring ventilation there, and safely recovering the bodies of the eleven miners that were still lying at the intersection of the Southeast Mains and 2 Left – 2 Southeast track. Scotia management asked the miners for volunteers and the three teams quickly filled up with willing miners for those three teams. My co-worker and friend Mike Halcomb was on one Scotia team formed in the 1980's and his was typical of the three original 1976 teams:

Ronnie Biggerstaff – Trainer

Mike Sparks – Captain

Randy Watts – Map Man

John Richardson – Gas Man and Stretcher Man

Mike Halcomb – Gas Man and stretcher Man

Joey Yonts – Communications Man

Dale Jackson – Gas Man or Extra and Dragger Apparatus Expert

Bob Childers – Communications and Coordinator

Mike Pease – Extra

There was some controversy concerning the Scotia safety director being appointed the leader of the #1 rescue team when being organized to do the recovery of the mine and the eleven bodies still inside the mine. The Mining Enforcement and Safety Administration (MESA) said that the agency intended to try to remove him from the list of those who will enter the mine because of his absence of mining experience and mining knowledge. This fact was revealed by his testimony given in the Department of Interior hearings into the Scotia disasters.

The hearings revealed that he had never worked as a coal miner and his seven years at Scotia had all been spent as safety director. Furthermore, his only training in mining had come from courses on use of safety equipment by the State Department of Mines and Minerals and one course on the use of a breathing apparatus given by MESA

He had a "very little, just a very little" familiarity with the layout of 2 Southeast Mains, where the eleven bodies were to be removed. He did not know how to properly test a self-rescuer until about three weeks after the twin explosions and did not "know the details really" of the ventilation of the Scotia mine. As well, the safety director was then under investigation by the Department of Interior for his actions prior to the explosions.[16]

After the organizing and equipping of the newly formed rescue teams, they began training for the rigorous and very dangerous work they would be facing when the #1 mine seals were broken and they began their recovery work. They could be seen in training, trudging up the steep hills of the Scotia complex while wearing their heavy,(30#) Dragger apparatus, with face masks on in the hot May and June weather of 1976.

At least two other Blue Diamond mines began forming and training their own rescue teams in the wake of the explosions, including Blue Diamond's Leatherwood and Justice mines.

On Sunday night, June 20, 1976, relatives of the 11 men killed on March 11 blocked the entrance to Scotia property in in an effort to force company and federal officials to speed up efforts to recover the bodies. Their efforts managed to stop production at the three Scotia mines that were still producing coal and where about 400 men were working.

Two days later, on the evening of Tuesday, June 22, a group of disgruntled miners confronted the group

---

[16] The Mountain Eagle, June 14, 1976.

of 20-25 pickets and crossed the picket line. That evening full production resumed in the Scotia upper mines.

The relatives of the 11 men killed in the second explosion formed the picket line after learning Friday, the 18th of June that Scotia and their parent company, Blue Diamond Coal, along with the Federal Mining and Enforcement Administration, (MESA) planned to unseal the mine in mid-July and that it would probably take months before the bodies could be recovered.

The relatives were determined to close Scotia until either the Company or MESA submitted a plan that would quicken recovery. Negotiations between the relatives, Scotia Employees Association President David McKnight and company officials produced no change in plans.

On Sunday night when the picket line was formed, the Scotia workers were understanding of the relatives' frustration and concern with the mine recovery plan and both groups stood together and discussed the explosions and the proposed plan to recover the mine in July. By Tuesday the mood of the Scotia miners had changed and the pickets were alone on the picket line. They couldn't understand why they should be put out of work over a decision made by Scotia and MESA.

"I only had two more weeks of training," said a man who was training to reenter the mine. *"Now that we got the rescue teams they (the relatives) throw up a picket line. They sure put a cork in it."* A miner's wife added, *"These men don't have anything to do with it."*

The group complained that the relatives were keeping them from making a living. They said the widows on the picket line were taken care of with food stamps and death benefits and didn't have to worry with such things. Another miner drove up and said, *"Something has got to bleed or blister. I'm not fooling with this bunch in the morning."*

An hour before the second shift was due to enter the mine at 2:00 p.m. some 40 women and men walked down the road and stood in front of the pickets. The anger that had built up on both sides now came together; the accusations were made: *"Whoever doesn't have a heart, go get your dinner buckets and go to work,"* a picket said after a few minutes of discussion. Within minutes a green pickup truck drove to the picket line, three men jumped in on the bed, and the vehicle continued on across the bridge and up the hill to the mines.

"They volunteered for the work," a miner's wife yelled. *"That's the chance they take."* The widows asked for understanding, *"Let'em go,"* a picket said as another

truck with three more in the back drove through. "*We'll remember you,*" the pickets yelled at each passing car or truck. By late afternoon the Scotia Coal Company had called its men back to work.[17]

Friends and Relatives of the miners sealed inside the Scotia mine had learned of the proposed plan to reenter the mine from an announcement made by federal, state, and company officials on June 18. The proposed plan was to renter the mine on July 14, by the driftmouth and that the bodies may not be reached for months.

The plan to enter through the driftmouth was devised by Scotia's parent firm, the Blue Diamond Coal Company, and approved by the Mining and Enforcement and Safety Administration (MESA.), the Scotia Employees Association, and the state Department of Mines and Minerals. The plan came under attack by the relatives of the dead men. They argued that the bodies could be recovered quicker by entering the mine through the 13 foot diameter borehole located in Frank's Creek. Robert Barrett, MESA'S Administrator, and Jasper Cornett, vice president of operations for Blue Diamond Coal co. said both points of entry were discussed at a Knoxville, Tennessee meeting earlier in the month, but that the driftmouth entry was decided upon for safety and logistical

---

[17] The Mountain Eagle, June 24, 1976.

reasons. Both acknowledged that if the driftmouth plan failed or became too difficult that the borehole route would be taken.

Scotia Employees Association President David McKnight considered using his veto power as the representative of workers at Scotia to block the proposed plan to recover the 11 bodies entombed in the Scotia mine through the driftmouth. The alternate plan would be to enter the mine through the driftmouth, which was favored by some because it was considered a quicker route to reach the deceased miners.

In early May Widows of some of the men killed in the March explosions issued a statement about their husband's fellow miners *"who have not come forward with information they have"* about safety conditions at the mine. Part of the statement included the following: *"We cannot see why this disaster happened at Scotia. We cannot see why Scotia management allowed it to happen. We believe there has been no management at Scotia."*

Just a couple of weeks after the upper mines at Scotia began producing coal again federal mine inspectors issued 67 citations, including six closure orders. Of the six closure orders, two were for improper grounding of electrical equipment, three were face equipment violations, and one closure order was issued of failure to follow the roof control plan.

A closure (104(c) required the withdrawal of all workers except those needed to correct the conditions and prohibited the workers from re-entering the mine or using the equipment until an inspection has been made and conditions are satisfactory as found by the inspection.

One positive change noted by inspector's reports was that Scotia now seemed to be emphasizing mine safety. Scotia's Safety Director reportedly called one working section's crew together and held a safety meeting and informed the crew that if they could not mine coal safe, to "pack their buckets and go to the office." It was not reported whether anyone did so.

On May 18, the Scotia Employees Association voted to strike the Scotia mines over a dispute involving the firing of two miners. Over half of the union employees voted in favor of the strike to support two miners accused by the company of smoking in the mines and fired by mine Superintendent Freddie Maggard.(Smoking underground in a coal mine was, and is, prohibited by State and Federal law.) David McKnight, (Scotia Employees Association President), stated that the strike was called because company officials did not follow company dismissal procedures. McKnight said the two men were fired by Superintendent Maggard before any discussion between a union committee and company officials could take place. McKnight maintained that conferences with the section foreman and mine foreman should have preceded the firing. He also stated that no written notice was given before the firings.

Jasper Cornett, the Vice President in charge of operations for Blue Diamond Company, said that the company had "discharged two men for smoking underground," and that there was a grievance procedure outlined in the contract but that it "is not being followed" by the union. McKnight followed by saying that, "the Scotia Employees Association wants the men put back to work."

Just 24 hours after the miners voted to strike, the men voted to end the walk-out and went back to work. The case was then submitted to the federal National Labor Relations Board for arbitration.

U.S. Steel Mine Rescue Team at Scotia Mine March, 9, 1976 – Photo Courtesy of Kenton County Public Library, Covington, Kentucky.

Family and Friends at Gravesite of Scotia Miner
Killed in Explosion

Courtesy of Kenton County Public Library,
Covington, Kentucky

Mike Halcomb: Scotia Rescue Team. Photos of Scotia Underground Mine, Scotia Rescue Teams, and Tipple Courtesy of Mike Halcomb, Former Scotia Miner.

Scotia Tipple

Eddie Nickels with Six Ton Locomotive inside
Scotia Imboden #1 Mine

Scotia Miner Mike Halcomb Building Cribs for Scotia Longwall

Scotia Miners Roger Bowman and Mike Halcomb

In Deck of New Taggart Locomotive

Members of Scotia Mine Rescue Team

Scotia Miner

Don Caudill with 2-6 Ton Locomotives

BLACK MOUNTAIN ELEGY

Scotia Mine Rescue Team with Trophy

From Left Front – Bob Childers, Mike Halcomb, Mike Sparks, Ronnie Biggerstaft, John Richardson, Dale Jackson.

In rear – Randy Watts, Joey Yonts, Mike Pease

Scotia 386' Bore Hole Under construction, 1976
Photo courtesy of the Kenton County Public Library, Covington, Kentucky.

News Conference after Scotia Mine Explosion Courtesy of Kenton County Public Library, Covington, Kentucky.

1976 Explosion Area – Scotia Mine

U.S. Dept. of the Interior

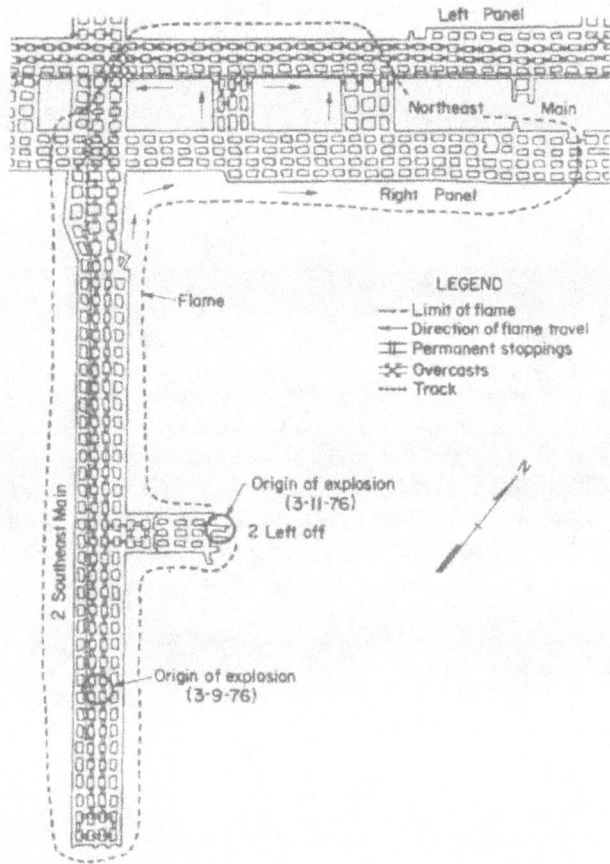

FIGURE 13. - Explosion area, Scotia Mine, Whitesburg, KY, March 9 and 11, 1976.

Eddie Nickels, Scotia Miner, with 6 Ton

Locomotive

Scotia Mine – Slope Portal

Scotia Tipple, Bathhouse, and Slope Portal,

Pine Mountain on Left of Photo,

Black Mountain on Right of Photo

Mike Halcomb – Bad Roof Conditions, Scotia #1
Mine

CHAPTER SEVENTEEN

With the addition of some of the miners that had been working in the now sealed #1 Scotia mine, the upper Scotia mines had plenty of help to begin producing coal again. When a miner had to take a day off there was always an extra man (or woman) to replace him or her on their piece of machinery, on the beltline, or outside on the supply storage area. The extra help was especially pleasing to my motor buddy and me, because having an extra man along to help load supplies on the yard, then ride shotgun on the locomotives inside the mine and to help unload the supplies, made our job much easier than when we had to work alone. It also made putting a rail vehicle back on the track when wrecked easier and faster to accomplish.

The coal produced by the upper mines was enough to load a 100 car unit train occasionally but the stockpile of coal diminished considerably quicker than when the #1 mine was producing their 2,500 tons daily. Both the Scotia miners and Scotia management were not only anxious to retrieve the entombed 11 miners from the mine but also looked forward to having their co-workers recalled from layoff caused by the explosions. Coal mines have always had to endure coal "booms and busts" and the miner's families have always had to bear the burden of hard times in the mines. Of course having to face "hard times" is nothing like having to carry the burden of losing a loved one in the mines. After the twin explosions at Scotia 26 families would carry that burden forever.

On the home front, I had been teaching my wife to drive before the explosions caused an interruption in that endeavor for a few months. Eventually she got her nerve up to take the driving test and I drove with her to Whitesburg, even though her driving skills were, shall we say, limited at best. She managed to pass the test the first time and needle me because it had taken me three times to pass the driving test.

I had insisted that she learn to drive, even though she had been reluctant, to say the least. When behind the wheel of the car, she would grip the steering wheel as if she was hanging on to a life jacket for dear life. Her knuckles would turn white and she would be near tears the whole time she was driving. So if I say I was surprised she managed to get her license on the first try, I kid you not.

A short time later she asked me *"What good is it to have a driver's license and not have a car of my own to drive?" What if one of the kids gets sick, how am I supposed to get them to a hospital without a car"* I couldn't argue with her with that logical reasoning, so one Saturday morning we climbed into my old work car and traveled across Sandlick mountain to Harlow Motor Company in Whitesburg.

After looking at several different cars Wanda decided she wanted the new 1976 Ford Elite that was in the showroom. We soon negotiated a little better deal than the sticker price, ($6,500.00), and she had her new car. I still worried about her driving skills but after a few weeks of worrying I settled my mind a little, thinking that maybe I was worrying myself to death over nothing.

Being on the second shift I left home in the daylight and got back home after dark. One night I arrived home around 11:30 p.m. as usual and noticed Wanda's car was parked facing the house instead of her usual backing in the driveway. Also I saw we had company. My dad and mom's car was in the driveway. This wasn't unusual but the lateness of the hour caused me some concern as I got out of the car. They never visited us that late. I wondered what might be wrong.

Opening the door and entering the living room I saw that my wife and kids were sitting there chatting with mom and dad. Everything seemed normal, so I then relaxed my fears and joined in the chat.

183

I sat there awhile and then I remembered to ask her, *"Wanda, why did you park the car differently today? You always back it in, what made you decide to pull in straight this time?* She glanced at my parents, then replied, *"Because I didn't want you to see the driver's side of the car."* I let that soak into my brain, then finally got the nerve to ask, *"What happened to the driver's side of your car?"*

It was then that she confessed that she had been going over Sandlick mountain and met a truck in a narrow section of the road and they collided. The whole side of the new car was heavily damaged but the car was still drivable. I was too glad that neither she nor one of our three kids was injured in any way to be angry about the car. She blamed the other driver but I gave him some benefit of the doubt since she was practically a novice driver. My mom and dad had come by to make sure they were alright after the accident.

After spending a few days in the body shop at Harlow's, it came back to us as good as new until Wanda put it in a ditch line a few years later. But that's another story.

In May 1976, MESA officials gathered in their Whitesburg, Kentucky office with the widows of the eleven men still lying at 2 South Mains in the Scotia mine to brief them on the mine conditions. They informed the widows that "the danger of another explosion was too great at this time" to take a chance on opening it. The official said he couldn't predict when the mine might be unsealed. When the decision was made to seal the mine on March 13, the estimate was that in 60 to 90 days the mine would be reopened.

On June 17, 1976, federal, state, company, and union officials announced that the mine would be unsealed on July 14th. They said the recovery teams planned to enter through the belt-line driftmouth located near the bathhouse and that it would likely take months to reach the bodies.

Relatives and friends of the dead miners were upset at the announcement of going through the driftmouth instead of going through the borehole, which was only about 4,000 feet from the bodies instead of the 4 to 4 1/2 miles the driftmouth route would have to travel. Robert Barrett, M.E.A.A.'S Administrator, and Jasper Cornett, Vice President for Operations at Blue Diamond, told the group that both points of entry were discussed at a Knoxville meeting earlier that month and that the driftmouth entry was decided upon for safety and logistical reasons. Both acknowledged that if the driftmouth

185

plan failed or became too difficult that the borehole route would be taken instead.

After the date of July 14th was decided on, preparations for the unsealing were being made to have three shifts of volunteer miners to back up the two Scotia Rescue Teams that would be tasked to work their way through the mine and recover the bodies. The Rescue teams would have to work under oxygen to explore the mine areas and build seals every seals every 500 feet or so; then the "fresh air crew" would come in afterwards and build backup seals to provide a double seal to assure that no toxic gases would leak from the seals.

The two Scotia rescue teams were still training for the unsealing when the word was spread among the miners that volunteers were needed to back up the two rescue teams when the bottom mine was unsealed. I didn't volunteer at first because my wife wasn't fully on board with the idea of me going into a mine that had been proven was so highly dangerous even in the best of times. Her uneasiness over the thought of me working in such a gassy mine, especially one that had been sealed for over four months, caused me to hesitate to add my name to the list.

I continued working at New Taggart for a while longer, still not sure what I wanted to do. After thinking it over a couple of weeks I thought to myself that if it was me lying in that dark and coal mine all this time that I would want my family to be able to have some piece of mind and some closure of the events of March 11th, 1976,

Finally, after days of mulling it over I expressed to Wanda that I felt I should volunteer to help bring the bodies out of the bottom mine. She argued the matter with me a little bit but eventually agreed, saying, *"Go ahead, you're going to do what you want to anyway."* She was right of course, so the next day I asked our new boss, Jimmy Adams, to call the mine office and put my name on the list. Afterwards, those of us volunteering for the fresh air crew had to wait until the concrete seals of the closed Scotia bottom mine were opened.

CHAPTER EIGHTEEN

Wednesday, July 14, 1976 was the date set by the Management of Blue Diamond Coal Company and the Federal Mine Enforcement and Safety Administration (MESA.), to break through the concrete seals and re-enter Blue Diamond's Scotia #1 Imboden seam mine.

The bodies of the eight Scotia coal miners and the three federal inspectors killed by the second explosion had now been sealed for over four months to give the dangerous conditions time to stabilize somewhat and to reduce the danger of more explosions and mine fires.

Officials expected the recovery to take around two months to reach the bodies but were aware that more time could be required if the conditions encountered slowed down the rescue teams. Roof falls and accumulations of water that must be pumped out when encountered, along with unstable roof conditions, were among the dangers expected to cause long delays while advancing through the mine. Ventilation would have to be reconstructed or restored and pockets of methane gas must be diluted with fresh air, and rendered harmless.

Jack Crawford, MESA.'S No. 2 man, described the men going into the mine as combined "rescue, recovery, and modified construction teams." Crawford, who was responsible for rescue and recovery problems that developed in the nation's coal mines, planned to be "in and out" of Cumberland, Kentucky during the recovery operations. When asked how long the recovery operations might take he said, "I don't know, this has turned out to be a whole lot slower than we anticipated." [18]

When sealed on March 19, two rows of concrete blocks with a porous fill material had been used to block al the entries into the Scotia #1 mine. To break through the two rows of blocks was made more difficult by the fact that regular drilling equipment could not be used because of the possibility that another explosion could be set off. The workers had to wear oxygen tanks and use only soft, non-sparking drill bits to break through the concrete blocks.

In the beginning, it was expected that it would take only a few hours to break through the seals but it ended up taking two days to very carefully break through the seals and measure the mine atmosphere at the portal. On Thursday, July 16, the first small holes were successfully drilled through. When measured through the holes the atmosphere was found to contain only two tenths of one percent methane, much below the five per-

---

[18] Mountain Life and Work, July, 1976.

cent needed to be explosive. After testing, heavier equipment was then used to break away the concrete seals.

The plan was for the three newly organized and trained Scotia Rescue Teams was to advance 500 feet at a time, under oxygen with their 30# Dragger apparatus, checking the atmosphere as they slowly advanced, while establishing ventilation controls. The teams would only be able to work one hour at a time.

As they progressed 500 feet they would then set up temporary "stoppings" made of wood braces and brattice cloth. Fresh air was then allowed into this 500 foot area to sweep the air of harmful methane into the return air. When the 500 foot move up was ventilated with fresh air, the fresh air work crew,(commonly referred to as the "Bull Crew" by the workers, came in behind the rescue team to build another temporary stopping in the same entry the rescue team had built theirs, to back up the first stopping. An access door would be built into the track entry temporary stoppings to allow access to the next 500 foot advance. The other three entries leading into the mine also had to have temporary stoppings built and backed up by the Bull Crew, but no doors were built in them.

L.D. Phillips, District Manager for the Federal Mining Enforcement and Enforcement Administration, which was monitoring the recovery efforts by Scotia, said the officials of the agency were " keeping them (the rescue team) in sight" when they began to explore the first part of the mine behind the seals, but did not enter the mine with the six man rescue team.

Mr. Phillips reported "no abnormal conditions" in the mine section that the rescuers entered and that as a result, the men were able to penetrate 2,000 feet into the shaft, where other seals shut off the rest of the mine. The section explored by the rescuers was ventilated for two hours before being entered, although the methane level was low there, about 1 percent.

Mr. Phillips said the rescue workers were jubilant at having finally entered the mine after two frustrating days of chipping away at the concrete seals that had initially expected to breach in about half a day.

He also said that the mine appeared in good shape in the first 2,000 feet, with no problems with the roof or mine floor. "So far, he said, they've just walked in there.[19]

Company officials had feared a similar demonstration on the scheduled opening date of July 14 and in preparation had moved the guard shack from the side of

_____

[19] New York Times, July 16, 1976.

the mountain at the mine entrance to a few hundred feet from Ky. 119 which runs in front of the mine. They also erected a new 8 foot high gate which barred anyone from driving onto the mine property unless the armed guard allowed entrance. Scotia officials had invited the families of the eleven miners still sealed inside the mine to attend the reopening of the seals but only relatives of two of the miners came to the mine. They allowed the family members to pass through the gate and go to a trailer, (the Scotia safety trailer), near the bathhouse. There, an employee of Blue Diamond Coal, Alan Blevins, told relatives they could come to the mine each week for a progress report, or the company would call them each week. The relatives indicated they preferred to have the company call them instead.

One big question was who would be in charge of the recovery operation? MESA was in charge of the mine at the time of the second explosion and Scotia was running the mine at the time of the first. Throughout the investigations of the disasters, the company and federal government had tossed the blame back and forth for the second explosion. Ralph Dye, the public Information officer for Blue Diamond Coal Company and Scotia Coal

Company said, "I don't know who is really in charge. Ask Jack Crawford," (MESA's #2 man). [20]

With the reopening of the mine and the advancing into the mine 2,000 feet with any major problems encountered and the first seals being successfully erected, the ventilation of that area of the mine could be ventilated and the fresh air crew could now go in and build another set of seals to back up the ones the rescue team had built.

---

[20] Mountain Life and Work, July, 1976.

CHAPTER NINETEEN

After the unsealing of the Scotia bottom mine, I arrived at work one evening around July 19, and my boss, Jimmy Adams, called me inside the mine office. He informed me that if I was still interested in going to the bottom mine to join the fresh air crews being assembled that I needed to report to the bathhouse where the communications center for the bull crew and the rescue teams were located.

I was directed to report to Bruce Jones, my former boss at New Taggart and who was now in charge of the second shift bull crew being assembled. A day shift and third shift crew was also put together the same day as they reported for their regular shift's work.

Having worked for Bruce Jones before, when he was the New Taggart second shift assistant mine foreman, I was very pleased to have him as a boss again. He was always fair to his men, was easy to work for and highly respected by his fellow miners and supervisors.

Around 12-15 second shift workers gathered in the dispatcher's office as we reported that evening, eager to hear what we would be doing to help retrieve the bodies and reopen the whole mine. We were told to watch out for each other when inside the mine since the four month closure might have resulted in some unsafe conditions that hadn't yet been observed or discovered. The first set of seals and the 2,000 foot initial advance had went very well and the hope was that we could move quickly deep into the mine and recover the bodies.

Bruce emphasized that although the families, the State, the Federals, and the Company wanted to reach the bodies as quickly as possible, they absolutely wanted to do so safely, without getting anyone else hurt or killed in doing so. We would have at least one company supervisor with us at all times and possibly at least one State or Federal Inspector would accompany us at all times.

He said that only brass tools would be used when working in an area where even the smallest amount of methane was present and that if and when we encountered one percent or more methane no work would be done until the area could be ventilated and the methane diluted with fresh air. As for the oxygen levels, it was stated that there might be occasions where we would have to work in lower than 20 percent oxygen, but if that happened, the air would be constantly monitored and if the air reached lower than 16 percent no work would proceed until the oxygen level was improved.

After the safety meeting, Bruce explained the layout of the first 2,000 foot section of the mine that had been explored and seals built by the rescue teams. We were tasked with going inside the mine and building the backup seals the rescue teams had built and with cutting any steel water lines and steel rails lying out by the seals. This was done as a safety measure to prevent any electrical current or outside lightning strike from traveling the steel inside the mine and possibly causing another explosion beyond the explored area.

With all the formalities taken care of and after a long safety meeting ended, we were assigned to 4-man teams and told that the slope track entry had been opened up also and that we could ride inside the mine on buses. The buses had been used in the bottom mine for years for mantrips. I had observed them going in and coming out of the mine before the explosions of March 9 and 11, but had never ridden one. We had always used "low-vein" steel mantrips pulled by a locomotive on each end of the mantrip at the upper mines. The buses could be operated from either end and each end could hold four miners, five if squeezed tightly enough. When working as a miner in later years after the bodies were removed and the mine producing coal again, I had many occasions to be in the deck of a bus and listen as the miners were so scrunched up they cursed and black-guarded like a bunch of sailors (or marines) on liberty. If however, they were headed outside the mine, I believe they would have tolerated 8 or 10 in one cab without complaint. Coal miners like being inside a mine but they LOVE being outside a mine. I'm speaking from personal experience here you know.

We loaded into the buses and proceeded slowly down the steep slope track with the bus's sand boxes open and sanding the tracks as we went along. We came to the first runaway switch just a few yards before entering the slope driftmouth. The miner sitting near the open door of the bus jumped out and switched the track to the straight and when we cleared the switch, he threw the switch back and jumped back in the bus and we slowly entered the driftmouth.

I had never been inside the Imboden seam of coal before but had heard many talk of the high coal there and how you could stand up anywhere and walk without having to bend over, which was a luxury in about any Eastern Kentucky mine. They hadn't lied. The first thing I observed was that the coal height was at least seven feet high and that it angled downward sharply, even more steeply than the hill we came down from the outside.

About 200 feet on down the steep entry was another runaway switch that would throw you into a deep hole if you were unlucky enough to lose control of the bus or locomotive and supply cars you were bringing into the mine. In all the years I later worked in that mine, I never took a locomotive or bus down that slope unless my sanders were working. Your life depended on it.

I saw many track vehicles wreck or wrecked on the switch located just outside the driftmouth at Scotia but I thank God I never wrecked or saw anyone that wrecked on the one inside the mine. If they had and was unable to exit or jump off the vehicle they would have been seriously injured or killed for sure.

Beyond that second switch was the steepest hill I had ever seen or would ever see inside a coal mine. It dropped straight down into the mine, but fortunately the steep hill was only about 500 feet long. At the foot of that treacherous slope was another switch which allowed access to an underground charging station which was where many track vehicle operators could charge their bus or locomotive batteries before trying to climb the steep slope to the outside. The 4 & ½ to 5 mile distance to the far reaches of the Imboden mine usually resulted in weak or dead batteries when returning to the bottom of the slope. To attempt that hill would be useless and foolhardy without at least half charged batteries or another locomotive to push you, (which was resorted to quite often.)

When we had traveled the 2,000 feet to the first seal my companions and I climbed from the yellow bus and as I looked around I saw that we were about 100 yards away from the seal in the track entry we were in. The crew I had been assigned to that day consisted of Hargus Maggard, James Miles, Steven Miles, and me. They were classified repairmen and this was our first meeting since they had always worked in the bottom mine and I had always been a "low coal" man working under Big Black Mountain at New Taggart. Of course the Imboden seal was underneath Big Black Mountain also and underneath the water table which made Scotia's #1 mine so gassy and so dangerous.

I didn't know it that day but I was to spend the next 16 years working with and around these three men, in some capacity, either during the recovery of the bodies or while producing coal. They were always willing to help with a job and were great to work with.

Hargus was our supervisor that first day and he began by assigning me to the two steel rails nearest the seal the rescue team had built. My job was to unbolt the fish plates holding the steel rails together. After unbolting them we used rail tongs (we called them rail dogs) to move the rails aside on the ribs. They would be re-laid when the next 500 foot move up was made and the rails near that next move would then be unbolted and moved.

When we finished that job we began the process of cleaning out the coal from the bottom and sides (ribs) of the area we had removed the rails from. Our seal would be built about 20 feet from the rescue team's seal, in the same cross-cut, and like the one they built, have a man-door built into it. The man doors were built into the track entry seals so that the rescue teams could access the next move up area and explore it while under oxygen. The seal we were building would in effect create an air lock between the two seals where the rescue teams could go between the seals and don their apparatus before using the second door to access the area to be explored. A rescue team member would be stationed at the first seal as an extra man and monitoring the team when exploring was being done by other members of the team.

In order to have an airtight seal it was necessary to shovel the ribs all the way to the solid of the block of coal. That was a harder task than might be expected because the ribs usually had to be shoveled to a depth of three or four feet until solid coal could be reached.

Working inside the crosscut maybe 20 or 30 feet from the fresh air made for a hot job and plenty of sweat flowing after a few minutes of shoveling. The sweat when mixed with the coal dust that was swirling around made for an atmosphere that was barely breathable as you worked. Usually a pick was a necessary tool to make sure you had reached solid coal when shoveling. One hates to think of what could have happened if one seal or both happened to have a fall of coal or rock at the sides of a seal which would not only short-circuit the mine air, but would likely allow an explosive mixture of oxygen and methane to exist in the atmosphere. This was one job that could not be allowed to be sloppy or half done. Every man's life depended on safe seals, safe workers and plenty of methane checks and air readings while exploring and working.

While our crew was working on our seal, others were working on the other three seals to be built in the other three entries. The entries being only about 90 feet apart allowed us to hear their loud voices and remarks while they were working. As each seal was finished, the crew that was finished moved to another to help the crew that was still busily working.

When dinner time came we all gathered at the track seal to spend our 30 minutes eating and getting acquainted. I knew most of the men from New Taggart but a few were from the bottom mine who I knew from sight only. Some I remember from those days were Paul Kemplin, Tommy Gross, Brad Whitaker, Charlie Davidson, Mike "Greenie" Sullivan, Ellis Hill, and Wayne Wilson, all who were dedicated miners who were anxious to help in retrieving those eleven miners.

We were aware when volunteering that our shifts would be 12 hour shifts, seven days a week until the bodies were recovered, no matter how long it took to accomplish the job. The estimate of two months by Company, State, and Federal officials was much too optimistic as was realized after the first two or three 500 foot advances into the mine. There was too much water to pump, too many stoppings had to be repaired or rebuilt, too many supplies had to be brought inside the mine for the building of the seals with every move up, and advancing into the mine had too many dangers involved to move too hastily.

I remember one incident where Mr. Tallman, the ventilation and mine recovery expert hired by Scotia to oversee the recovery, wanted our crew to knock out a concrete block stopping in some old works of the mine. Tallman personally directed three or four of us to help him with the job. The stopping was located several breaks from the main line and was built about 50' inside the crosscut. When we reached the last open crosscut Tallman directed that one of us at a time enter the cross-cut with a sledge hammer with a brass head and knock as many blocks out as we could until we tired, when we were to come out of the crosscut and another man would take his turn at swinging the hammer.

I wondered, as we squatted there listening to his instructions, why all the caution was necessary to knock one 7'x 22' stopping which Tallman thought would take four men to accomplish. I soon found out when I took the first turn. I walked up to the stopping and immedi-ately noticed that the oxygen level in the immediate area of the stopping was very low, causing me to breath heavi-ly even before I struck the first blow with the hammer.

As I swung the hammer with the first blow, I felt weak and dizzy and felt as though I might pass out. After only 4 or 5 swings I knew I had to get back into fresh air or pass out. Tallman could see I was struggling and shouted "Come on out of there my man, someone else will take their turn now!" I stumbled out of the crosscut, wondering why I was so confused and woozy. I slumped down beside the men waiting in the fresh air of the open crosscut while the new hammer man was at the stopping and we observed him having the same reaction I had experienced. Three or four swings of the sledgehammer were all he could manage also and he stumbled back to where we were waiting.

One of us asked him, "Mr. Tallman", (he was a retired miner and probably in his 60's at that time,) what's the oxygen level near that stopping?" He grinned as he replied, "There's only 16 percent oxygen at the stopping, which is sufficient and safe enough to breathe, but makes swinging the hammer a harder chore. It's perfectly safe, just hit as many licks as you can and come back out and another man will replace you. This has to be done to improve ventilation in this area."

We managed to finish the job after taking several turns at swinging the 16 # hammer which seemed to weigh 60# in the low oxygen level experienced when near the stopping. Even knocking the stopping completely out didn't seem to improve air flow after it was completely leveled. I assume Mr. Tallman knew what he was doing, since he was the supposed ventilation expert who was paid $500.00 per day (worth $2,442.43 in 2021) to oversee the restoring of the mine ventilation as the teams advanced towards the eleven fallen miners.

CHAPTER TWENTY

By the end of July, 1976, Scotia Rescue teams and the fresh air crews had reached about 3,500 feet into the mine, a little over half a mile, with 4 miles or more remaining before reaching the bodies. No major disruptions to the advance had been encountered except for the areas of high methane and occasional pools of water that needed to be pumped.

After each 500 foot advance, the whole area had to be carefully monitored and conditions checked and at least eight seals had to be built before the next move up and exploration could be accomplished.

The two Scotia teams worked mostly on the day shift when conducting a 500 foot move into the mine, which was done along with several Federal and State mine inspectors who monitored the seals closely as the teams carried out their work. Occasionally an Inspector or two accompanied the rescue team as they explored a new area under oxygen. They were determined that the job of recovery went smoothly for all concerned, as was the Scotia and Blue Diamond officials.

Our fresh air crew also had at least one Federal Inspector assigned to monitor our progress each day, to make sure we did our work correctly, safely, and according to law. The use of safety glasses and gloves was highly monitored by the inspectors when working on building a seal, which required several 4x4 timbers and one inch lumber to be used in their construction. When hammering a nail the use of safety glasses was required and was the cause of a verbal warning if caught not wearing them.

None of us were adverse to having inspectors with us at all times. They were there to help, not impede our work. They were under some pressure to get the fallen men out of the mine and released to their families as soon as was safely possible. At the same time they and Company officials wanted no major incidents or major injuries to occur while recovery work was being done.

The Federal mine inspector assigned to my second shift crew was Inspector Rooney, from Pennsylvania. He often spoke of the disaster that happened in the Consol No. 9 mine in Farmington, West Virginia on November 20, 1968, that resulted in 78 miners killed in that series of fires and explosions. The initial explosion in that mine was followed by several secondary explosions for several days afterward. Inspector Rooney expressed his sorrow to us that some of those miners killed in that explosion were then (in 1976) still sealed inside that mine. He was as anxious to recover the bodies of the eleven Scotia miners as any of us but he wanted to make sure it was done safely.

The stress of working seven days a week in 10 hour shifts and many double shifts finally began to tell on some of the men in our crew. One of our crew became involved with a verbal altercation with our assigned inspector after finding a knife while building a seal. He had discovered the knife lying on the mine bottom under some loose coal and stuck the knife in his pocket until we could finish the seal and he could turn it over to the Federal Inspector. He then forgot about it and when someone mentioned to the inspector of the find he blew up because of the failure to turn the knife into his care. He had instructed that any interesting objects found while recovering the mine were to be turned over to him for safe keeping. The failure to do so caused an outburst from him that resulted in his being sent back to his home state after some of the miners objected to his actions. Stress on both sides was the likely cause of the whole unfortunate incident. Under normal circumstances an incident like this would have likely have never resulted in someone's removal from their job, but these were not normal circumstances.

The end of the month of August found that our teams had reached a little over 6,000 feet into the mine with the exploration and building of seals. One good thing was that no major roof falls had occurred while the mine was sealed, therefore saving lots of time and effort to remove the rock had any falls occurred. In fact, no evidence that the mine had ever suffered an explosion had been encountered as far as had already been explored. Even the rock dusting that had been done before the explosions was still evident on the mine roof, ribs, and bottom of the mine.

Each time a 500 foot move had been made and seals built, the track had been bolted back together, allowing the locomotives and supply cars to travel within a couple of hundred feet of the seals that were to be built with their load of lumber and five gallon buckets of sealant called, Regi-Pak. The sealant was a porous material that was used to apply to the yellow brattice cloth to cover any holes and tears in the cloth and around the top, bottom, and sides of the seal. This material required that anyone handling it or applying it needed to wear protective glasses and gloves before applying it to the seal. I always wore a protective face (dust) mask when inside the mine and shoveling or working in the face area where dust was always a problem. The sealant had a danger warning listed on the side of the bucket and made me wonder at the time if that porous substance might cause us some type of harm in the future. Regardless of the danger involved we had a job to do and we had to suck it up and go on. I often wonder if some inquiring mind might someday do an investigation as to the causes and effects of exposure to that chemical, whatever it was, that it contained that was so harmful.

My locomotive co-worker and I stayed especially busy during this first couple of months of the recovery, as we not only had to help build seals but were tasked with loading the supplies into the supply cars on the outside supply area (located near the main office) and then had to transport them inside. We spent a lot of time getting our sanders on the locomotives working each day as the moisture and water inside the mine often resulted in wet sand in the sand boxes of the locomotives and buses. No one, but no one, dared to tackle the slope entry with a track vehicle without all the sanders on the vehicle working unless they were a glutton for punishment or were a little stupid or both.

When I was engaged in taking a load of supplies or men around the curve across from the supply yard and pointed the nose of the locomotive down that darn slippery slope entry, the pucker factor was as extreme as it could get. I could just imagine going through that first runaway switch at full speed with a heavy load of supplies and hitting that wall of dirt of the high bank of the hillside. Or even worse, if the first runaway switch was safely negotiated, one could still start sliding and fly into the runaway switch located just before the steepest part of the slope. Being able to go outside the mine and enjoy the high top out there (the sky) was little payment for the hazard of having to travel back down that slope. I still have nightmares about it occasionally.

When recovery teams reached about 7,000 feet into the mine in late August-early September, the teams encountered much water that had to be pumped before teams could advance further into the mine. The track entry not only had water that had to be pumped but also larger amounts of methane and bad roof conditions were encountered. This slowed the recovery efforts considerably until the conditions could be corrected.

In the third week of September, 1976, Robert Barrett, Administrator of the federal Mining Enforcement and Safety Administration, stated that charges would "definitely" be brought against officials and employees of Scotia Coal Company. He also said that some charges "will go higher than the supervisory personnel."

Department of the Interior officials stated that no charges would be made until the entire mine is opened and the explosion site examined. No firm estimate had been made on when the on-site investigation would start, but delays in opening the mine make it doubtful that the investigation can begin before the first of the year.

Note: The justice department took more than three years to bring a criminal indictment against the company, naming no individuals for violations related to the disaster. In 1979 a six count criminal indictment was handed down by a federal grand jury in Catlettsburg, Kentucky charging Blue Diamond with the mine safety laws in connection with the second mine disaster.

In April, 1983, criminal charges were dropped against Blue Diamond Coal Co. in connection with the explosions of March 9 and 11, 1976. In the plea bargaining agreement, Scotia Coal Co. pleaded guilty to two criminal counts and pleated to no contest to three other counts contained in the June, 1979 federal indictment. In exchange for Scotia's guilty pleas, federal prosecutors agreed to drop all six charges against Scotia's parent company, Blue Diamond Coal Company. Under the agreement, Scotia pleaded guilty to:

- Failing to train each of its miners in the use of self-rescuing devices and

- Falsifying mine records about a pre-shift mine examination the company also pleaded no contest to charges that it

- Knowingly falsified mine ventilation maps to show ventilation devices appearing in places where there were none.

- Did not follow the approved ventilation plans for the #1 mine or properly control levels of methane and coal dust in the mine.

- Did not have a certified miner check or fireboss areas of the #1 mine for methane and for oxygen deficiency shortly before miners went to work on March 9.

On Tuesday, September 21, 1976, Dow Phillips , the chief Mining Enforcement and Safety Administration official at Scotia, announced that the teams had managed to travel 8,500 feet into the mine since the July, 14 unsealing. This was near the halfway point to the location of the bodies of the miners, about 10-12,000 feet to go to reach the bodies.

In October, 1976, a suit was filed in federal court in Knoxville, Tennessee, by the widows of the fifteen miners killed in the first explosion in the Scotia mine on March 9, 1976. The suit asked that Blue Diamond Coal

Company pay $30 million to compensate the widows for their husbands' deaths and asks another $30 million from the company in punitive damages for alleged company negligence in running the mine.

The suit maintained that Blue Diamond and Scotia did not maintain ventilation in its Scotia mine that would sweep explosive methane gas safely out of the mine. It also said that Blue Diamond did not follow acceptable safety procedures. The suit was handled by Gerald Stern and his colleague, George Frampton Jr., and they were assisted by attorneys James Asher of Whitesburg, Kentucky, Eugene Goss of Harlan, and J.D. Lee of Knoxville, Tennessee.

In August 1980, in the 15 widows' suit against Blue Diamond, an out-of-court settlement was reached which was expected to bring 10 to 12 million dollars in damages to 35 of the dead miners' survivors. The settlement gave tax-free lump sum payments and long-term annuities to the 13 surviving widows and the 22 children of 15 of the miners who died in the first explosion on March 9, 1976. The cash value divided among them, or the cost to Blue Diamond was $5.9 million. The company also agreed to pay back $400,000 that the widows had received in workers' compensation benefits should those payments be successfully challenged as a result of the negligence settlement.

Widows of the 11 men killed in the second explosion sued the federal government for $1.2 million each in damages and if an investigation should exonerate MESA. of blame in the disaster, they intended to file suit for $12 million.

Five years later, in 1981, the widows whose husbands were killed in the second explosion settled out-of-court with the federal government for a total of $2.1 million.

CHAPTER TWENTY ONE

Having reached the halfway point to the bodies, the going was a little better in the next stretch of mine. The water, bad mine roof, and the dangerous methane levels had been conquered and was in the past. Now the hope was for advancing to the bodies without too much difficulty. The teams, the Company, Federal, and State officials now hoped for better conditions as the explosion area was neared.

The whole month of October the teams found that conditions were not as bad as when we encountered so much water and other problems in September. The last week of October we reached a point where the going would be much slower, as we had reached the 2 South Mains and Northeast Mains switch and the next area of the mine would be explored carefully as we would be only a couple thousand feet from the Northeast Mains – 2 Southeast switch where the bodies of the miners were located.

The next 500 ft. move-up in early November brought us to within 1,600 feet of the bodies. This move was the point at which we also finally began to see stark evidence of the explosion of March 11. The roof, floor, and top of the mine was completely devoid of any rock dust and the darkness of the soot and coal dust made it difficult for our powerful wheat lights to penetrate the darkness. Only when the light beam was directly pointed at an object could one make out what was being illuminated. The darkness experienced when one turns the lights off in a darkened room doesn't come close to the intensity of the darkness of the entries that had been affected by the huge blast.

As we gingerly entered the area and were trying to acclimate our eyes to the scene around us, Brad Whitaker, one of my fellow fresh air workers, kicked at a slight mound of coal dust lying on the rib of the coal and when he raked it with his mining boot he exclaimed, "Hey guys, I've got a mining cap here!" We all gathered around him with much curiosity, as we knew that any object found in that area so close to the explosion area would require careful examination.

As he examined the mining hat he again exclaimed, "I see the name of the owner and it's the hat of a man killed in the explosion!" The explosion had carried the hat 1,500 feet from the 2 Southeast Mains and Northeast Mains switch where the bodies of the men and the two locomotives with their supply cars were when the explosion hit.

Other evidence of the explosion was displayed all around where the hat was found, all of which was difficult to make out until we raked the coal dust with our boots. Pieces of shredded paper littered the bottom of the entry, along with pop cans, pieces of plastic, snack food wrappers, and various odds and ends that the wind and pressure of the explosion picked up as it roared along the main track entry of 2 South Mains.

The area where the hat was found was the point where the force of the explosion had diminished and there was little evidence from that point of the mine to the Northeast Mains – 2 South Mains switch that an explosion had occurred.

An explanation to the reader here:

The names of the track switches are confusing at times because of their similarity, even to the coal miners that were otherwise familiar of the Scotia#1 mine.

The Northeast Mains – 2 Southeast Mains switch was the switch located where the eleven miners were killed in the explosion of March 11.

The Northeast Mains – 2 South Mains switch was the one closer to the outside (located 3 & ½ miles from the outside,) the switch where the mine phone was located that Rick Parker and Ernie Collins used to call the outside officials after escaping from the explosion of March 11, 1976.

Whitaker turned the hat that was found over to the federal inspector accompanying us and we stepped gingerly around the area to make sure we didn't inadvertently step on any evidence or more items belonging to the deceased miners we were trying to recover. The track entry was the only entry where we expected we might find further personal items, but to my knowledge, no other personal items were discovered that night.

We built our four seals that night with every man aware that our goal to recover the bodies was close to fulfillment and we couldn't let our guard down at this point. The mine was still dangerous as far as we knew. Every worker on the rescue teams and fresh air crews was well aware that there was a locomotive sitting at the head of 2 Southeast Mains with a compressor that "kicked on" when the pressure decreased on the brake system. We knew that we could only hope and pray that either the oxygen was too low or the methane levels too high at this point in time to create an explosion even if the compressor on that locomotive should still be active. It would only be when that section was explored and ventilation restored that the danger would be at the highest level possible.

Only two more moves remained after we finished our seals that night. The going from this point would have to be made much more slowly, with an abundance of caution from every man. We were at the serious stage, not meant for the faint-hearted. We didn't yet know what we might be called on to do in the coming days but it was on every man's mind. Would we be the ones who would be tasked with picking up the bodies and preparing them to be transported to the surface? We didn't yet know but the anxiety was stressful to the crew and the supervisors.

In this area of the mine the teams faced worsening gas problems and roof conditions. Increasing barometric pressure in the past few weeks was another worrying problem since increasing pressure meant more methane would be liberated from the mine ribs, top and bottom.

The rescue teams on their last advance had been advancing (under oxygen) in eight percent methane and 17 percent oxygen, which was worryingly close to the five percent of methane and 20 percent oxygen needed to be at the most volatile point.

Mine officials were concerned that the mine roof conditions in the recovery area could be bad. The roof in that area had been bolted with conventional (screw type) roof bolts instead of the resin bolts then used by Scotia.

The resin bolts were much better than conventional bolts and their holding power much better.

Scotia announced in early November that the bodies were expected to be recovered in a matter of weeks. They stated that the teams were working "in the most explosive range of gas you can find." [21] The announcements came at a meeting between the families of the men and officials of Blue Diamond and federal and state mining officials. The bodies were expected to be recovered within two to three weeks if no further obstacles were encountered.

Jasper Cornett, Vice President of Blue Diamond, stated at the time that six or seven representatives from the 11 miner's families would be allowed to accompany the final recovery teams. That group will include federal, state, company, and employee representatives, funeral home employees and a representative of the Letcher County coroner.

Cornett said that the recovery teams would ventilate the area before an attempt would be made to retrieve the bodies. Bodies were to be identified by the numbers on the batteries the men had carried and check-off numbers on their mining belts.

---

[21] The Mountain Eagle November 4, 1976.

The rescue teams were not only facing dangers due to mine conditions but were subject to another kind of danger from their apparatus they wore when exploring the mine. Three or four members of the rescue teams had to be removed from the recovery efforts because of tension or oxygen toxicity in their blood caused by use of their breathing apparatus.

On November 18, 1976, our fresh air crew went inside the mine to build backup seals around the bodies of the eleven miners. The rescue teams had finally reached the bodies and explored the area around them. They then built seals around the area and began the ventilation of the area.

Our job was to build backup seals all around the area without disturbing any evidence and without approaching the bodies that were scattered around the area. We built our seals using the same method we had followed all through the mine for five miles over the past four months, shoveling the coal to the bottom and the edges of the ribs, then using yellow brattice cloth, 1"x"10" inch boards, and regi-packs (referred to by us miners as mine foam) to cover areas of the seal where seals might occur.

We did all our work with the bodies clearly visible to us as they lay in the same position they had been lying for the past 253 days. No features were visible, only their mold covered bodies and the two locomotives and supply cars that were still sitting in the blackness of the destruction that surrounded the whole area.

The men worked with few words being spoken in respect to the deceased men around us. When talk was necessary, words were spoken in a whisper. The entire time I was working on those seals I was thinking how close I had come to being one of those mounds lying just a few feet from us. We worked frantically to complete at least double the seals we were used to building during a move-up. We had been instructed that officials were counting on us to complete the seals that night so they could be removed early in the morning.

It was 5:00 a.m. on Friday, the 19th of November before we completed all the seals around the bodies. We had been working 15 hours straight to complete them and our crew was totally exhausted by the labor and stress of those hours. We were under observation by federal and state inspectors the whole tine and many company officials were present, all who were urging us to work as quickly as possible to complete the job so the people waiting to recover the bodies could do their job.

Finally we arrived outside and as we came up the slope entry in the buses, we observed several people already gathered on the bridge spanning the gorge the track was in. After arriving on the surface I headed to the bathhouse and took a shower. Then the long wait began for the bodies to come out.

All the official party that were to be present at the recovery had gone into the mine as soon as we exited the mine. Those officials included Harold Kirkpatrick, Kentucky State Mining Commissioner, Robert Barrett, Mining Enforcement and Safety Administration (MESA), three pathologists, and representatives from five area funeral homes.

The day shift motor crew had gone ahead of the officials into the mine and the now familiar supply cars with a locomotive in front and one behind were going to be used once again to bring dead miners out of the mine. As had occurred with the victims of the first explosion, yellow brattice cloth lined the bottoms of the cars.

Twenty seven men entered the mine at 7:00 a.m. to begin the process necessary to bring the bodies outside. After arriving at the end of the track near the bodies, the medical team and pathologists examined the fallen miners before the funeral home employees made preparations to remove the bodies.

Inspectors from MESA mapped the area where the bodies lay and took photographs of the scene. They then gathered the personal effects of the miners.

Barrett, head of MESA, and Kirkpatrick, Kentucky Mining Commissioner, returned to the surface to brief family members and to speak with newsmen gathered outside Scotia property. They stated to the news people that it appeared that all eleven men died from the initial force of the explosion, although, Joe Cook, Assistant Administrator of MESA, reported that as many as three or four of the self-rescue devices were removed from the belts of the dead miners.

After the medical people and the federal and state officials completed their examination of the deceased miners and the surrounding area, they headed back to the surface, arriving there around 10:00 a.m. The locomotives and supply cars were still inside the mine preparing to transport the bodies to the surface.

I left the bathhouse and I and others began gathering on the steel bridge spanning across the slope track to the Scotia parking lot. Our view allowed us to watch the locomotives as they emerged from the mouth of the mine. We had a clear view of the track from the driftmouth all the way to the mine maintenance building, which had been set up as a temporary morgue to receive the deceased miners. From there they would be loaded into the different hearses waiting to receive the miners.

About eighty to a hundred people were gathered on the bridge when the first locomotive emerged from the mine. Like the first fifteen men brought out of the mine after the first explosion, the bodies were lying in the two supply cars covered with yellow brattice cloth.

As the locomotives proceeded slowly up the slope some waiting family members and friends of the miners there became emotional and expressed their feelings, some with moaning and others in tears with expressions of anguish directed at Scotia officials. *"Oh God!" "Oh Lord Jesus!" "I hope you're happy!" "I hope you rot in hell!" "Why they're in an old mine car covered with a sheet*, said one man. The shouts were directed at Scotia officials that were standing on one side of the bridge as the locomotive climbed the slope with their precious cargo. The feeling of the relatives and friends was understandable, as they had waited eight months and eight days for their loved ones to be recovered from the mine.

A few of those waiting had to be sedated by a nurse who was on the scene. Some others in the crowd hugged and comforted each other as tears rolled down their cheeks. Some tried to speak but the words wouldn't come. Even some of the waiting Scotia miners who had never even met the deceased eight miners and three federal inspectors under those bright yellow pieces of brattice cloth were trying to hide their faces as the tears rolled from their eyes. It was one of the saddest scenes one could ever imagine and one I'll never forget.

In early October Federal inspectors conducted a "blitz" inspection of the Upper Taggart mine, closing five sections for unsafe conditions and issued one citation for conditions that constituted "imminent danger." When a blitz inspection occurs, inspectors check each working section of a mine at the same time. In eight straight days of inspections, the mine was cited for 30 violations of mining laws by seven inspectors from MESA.

The inspectors found illegal amounts of loose coal and coal dust in every working section of Upper Taggart. Four closure orders were written on the basis of these violations. The imminent danger violation was also based on illegal amounts of loose coal and coal dust. The fifth closure order was issued because of inadequate ventilation in one of the sections.

When asked, Blue Diamond spokesman Ralph Dye said he would not comment on the violations but later labeled them frivolous violations. When informed of the closure orders and continued ventilation regulations, he amended his statement to say that "they certainly need corrective action." All the violations found at the Upper Taggart mine were eventually corrected.[22]

Tragically, one of the men involved in the effort to recover the eleven miners was killed in an automobile accident just a few days before the bodies were recovered. Clifford Darrell Rice, age 21, was killed when an empty coal truck swerved to miss a tractor – trailer, slid sideways and struck Rice's pickup. Neither the coal truck driver nor the driver of a jeep involved in the accident was injured .Rice had been working on the recovery team since July 14, when the seals were opened at Scotia #1 mine. The accident happened on Ky. 119 just a few miles south of the Scotia mine.

---

[22] The Mountain Eagle, November 25, 1976.

CHAPTER TWENTY TWO

Following the recovery of the eleven miners, the week of November 22 through November 26 was observed by Scotia workers as a moratorium in honor of the 26 men who died in the Scotia mine. It was a period of reflection and much needed rest for both the workers and management of Scotia and Blue Diamond Coal Company.

Since the opening of the sealed #1 mine on July 14, until November 19, when the bodies were recovered, the recovery work had proceeded 24 hours a day, seven days a week for the three shifts of rescue teams and fresh air crews. The stress of working in such dangerous conditions had not only affected the workers, but their families were affected also by the long days of worrying that their husbands and sons might end up having to be rescued themselves or recovered should another explosion occur while recovery work was going on.

My own wife and kids suffered from the stress of worrying about my own safety during that period of time. When their school began classes in August, I rarely got to see them because when I got home after midnight they were asleep and when they left for school I was asleep. All their concerns were expressed to their mom, who would relay them to me, causing me much worry at the time, but I knew that the stress in my family was nothing compared to the stress that the families of the entombed men had suffered and were still suffering, while waiting for us to recover their loved ones.

In December, 1976, MESA officials said that tests showed that methane levels had reached explosive proportions in a "massive" worked out portion of the mine and that another section was quickly reaching the point where the gas is combustible. Federal, State, and Company officials met at the mine site on December, 7th to grapple with the potentially explosive areas and to develop plans to reopen the remaining portions of the mine.

Throughout the recovery operation, the teams reopening the mine had had problems with unstable gas conditions and at one point teams were working in an explosive condition. The worked out area as tested showed a methane reading of 14.4 percent methane and 17 percent oxygen. Both were within the range of explosiveness, which is 5 to 15 percent methane and 12 to 20 percent oxygen.

Also tests made in the Northeast Mains section of the mine showed readings of 17.5 percent methane and 14.4 percent oxygen. MESA officials stated that the chances of the gas being ignited were "remote." They were however, worried about the presence of batteries in both sections that could produce sparks if they were to be disturbed by a roof fall. The batteries were installed to run a fire prevention spray system along the belt line.

MESA stated that the 2 Southeast Mains section, where the explosions originated, gas levels were holding steady at non-explosive levels. A MESA official stated that "We will not work rescue teams knowingly in explosive levels."

In the effort to recover the bodies, teams did, at times, work in explosive mixtures and once traveled 1,300 feet under oxygen to unhook batteries on the belt-line spray system and on other machinery before the area was ventilated.

When our fresh air crew returned to work at the #1 mine after the week off to honor the fallen miners, we began the process of preparing the mine for the producing of coal again. Our crew was taken about three miles from the slope portal to some old works where we would work to start the first section (1 West off South Mains Parallel) to produce coal after the recovery of the bodies.

We parked our mantrip bus on the main line, (South Mains) and proceeded into the old works near the track, testing methane and oxygen levels as we went. The air on the main line was very cold but the old works shielded us somewhat from the cold as long as one had a warm coat to wear. I remember feeling frozen all that day no matter how hard we worked.

Bruce Jones, the second shift foreman of the fresh air crew, (we had fresh air aplenty there for sure,) sent some members of our crew to bolt some bad roof in one entry, while he assigned me to operate a scoop. My job was to use the scoop to move very large mounds of coal from the area which had for some reason in the past been piled into several breaks instead of sent outside on the belt.

I spent the whole day half-frozen and eating gobs of coal dust stirred up by the scoop. I was wearing a face mask but plenty of dust still managed to sift through the mask and around the mask seals to enter the throat. By the end of the shift I had managed to remove the mounds of coal and transport them to another part of the old works. One consolation that day was that I knew I would be going home after my shift's work, unlike when we were recovering the bodies and one never knew when or what time you would be allowed to go home.

As the rescue teams continued their exploring of the mine, the 2 Left Panel was eventually explored and ventilated by the teams. At one point afterwards out crew was taken by bus to clean up and rock dust the area where the bodies had laid so long. We then had a chance to observe the destruction that had occurred even at that great distance, (about 2,500 feet) from the point of supposed ignition in 2 Southeast Mains.

The belt line coming out of that section was flipped upside down and the whole area was as "black as a dungeon" as the saying goes. Pieces of paper and plastic were actually lodged under the resin roof bolt plates where they had been driven by the force of the blast. Again we observed all kinds of miscellaneous items driven down the path of the explosions.

The block stopping near the 2 Southeast – Northeast Mains switch that had blown out partially was at that point still missing some concrete blocks. This was the stopping where I had observed a Scotia miner and two MSHA inspectors lying against while we were building seals around the night of Nov. 18 and 19. They were in the process of coming down the track after examining the sagging rock to be bolted up when the explosion's deadly force roared down from 2 Southeast Mains the night of March 11. The force of the explosion had blown them into the concrete stopping. This stopping was only a few feet from where Rick Parker and Ernie Collins were working when the explosion hit. It was truly a miracle that they survived that blast.

The explosive force of those two explosions was very evident when we viewed the 2 South Main belt head that John Hackworth had been manning when the first explosion happened. The blast coming from 2,500 foot away had upended the belt for the whole length of the belt line. It was evident to our crew while we were rock dusting that months of work remained before any coal production could be done in the two sections that were involved in the explosions.

By the end of January 1977, recovery teams had managed to re-ventilate all the area except the 2 Southeast section where the explosions were believed to have originated. Re-ventilation of that section could not begin until heavy rock dusting was completed in other portions of the mine.

In February the recovery operations were slowed by ice collecting on the slope and very low temperatures were affecting the batteries that operate equipment in the mine. I cannot express enough the miserable conditions our crew endured during that winter. We worked every night on the slope in below zero temperatures, chipping ice from the sides of the track where rivers of water coming down the slope had frozen and turned to ice. The ice was built up too high for supply cars and the buses to be able to go over without using a pick and shovel on the ice.

We used a supply car to shovel the ice into it and could only work 15 minutes at a time until we walked to the charging station at the bottom of the slope to warm ourselves around the power center located there. The temperature at one point reached -18 degrees and every coal miner knows that the temperature just inside the main air intake entry is always much colder than any-where else inside or outside the mine.

I'll never forget that cold winter in which we had to dress as if we were on a snowy mountain in Siberia instead of a coal mine in Kentucky. The whole winter of 1976-77, we spent a good deal of our time just chipping away at that ice on the steep slope entry of Scotia Coal Company.

In February, the 2 Left Panel had been explored and ventilated by the rescue teams and our crew was sent to do some clean up on that section. We side tracked our bus at the mouth of 2 Southeast and South Mains switch and walked the 2,000 feet to the 2 Left Panel sec-tion where 13 men had died in the first explosion.

As we walked along the track we observed the rock that had been the cause of the second group of men being caught in the second explosion. It had been finally bolted securely to the roof by the time we saw it. As I stopped to gaze at that rock and as our crew stood there and quietly talked among themselves about the infamous piece of stone, I realized for the first time that I had hate in my heart for a rock, of all things. If it hadn't been for that sagging boulder, eight Scotia miners and three federal inspectors would not have died. The fact that I was nearly one of those miners intensified my hate for it.

The destruction we saw on our way to the section was evident as we went along. Every foot of the way was a scene of destruction and darkness and as we neared the mouth of 2 Left Panel. When were arrived at the mouth of the section and turned up the track entry we noticed that rock dust was still visible on the ribs and top of the section. It was only 600 feet to the face of the section so it only took a few minutes to arrive there.

The first thing we saw on section was the 7,200 volt power box and the mine phone. Beside the phone was a tool box on which one of the miners had allegedly been sitting when the first explosion hit. We advanced on to the face area where six of the miners who had lived through the explosion had barricaded. They had at first tried to escape down the return entry with their self-rescuers opened and being used, but turned back after going 5 breaks and seeing nothing but smoke and destruction.

When they returned to the section they then barricaded and hoped for quick rescue. When the air in the barricade was exhausted they then perished. While there at the barricade we observed the materials they had used to build it, which consisted of rocks, blocks of coal and loose coal which had probably been scooped with their hands onto the bottom of the barricade, in hopes of keeping the good air from escaping. The yellow brattice cloth they had used was still hung from the roof bolts with nails and both sides of the yellow brattice cloth were unfastened and sagging loosely. It was a scene found just as the miners had left it from the day of the first explosion.

In one entry the roof bolter was still in the face area where the bolting crew was installing resin roof bolts when the mine exploded. A large rock was lying on the top of the roof bolting machine where it had fell from the roof. The rock was about 3 foot wide and approximately 4 foot long.

MESA. officials had expressed one theory that the second explosion was caused by that rock sparking as it fell onto the roof bolter and igniting methane that had likely saturated the area after the first explosion destroyed the ventilation on the section. After I saw the bolter and rock with my own eyes I fully discounted that the rock caused the explosion. It was plain to see that all the roof bolts normally carried loosely on the roof bolter were still there and barely moved around. If an explosion had originated anywhere close to the bolter the bolts would have been scattered for dozens of yards from the force of the blast. They had barely moved and the rock's falling had caused little more than a slight jolt when it hit the bolting machine, the roof in that section being only six feet in height.

In March, 1977, recovery teams finished ventilating the area and reached the two locomotives, one of which was believed to have caused the two explosions that killed the 26 men on March 9 and 11, 1976. Two electricians, accompanying the rescue teams cut the leads leading to the batteries that operated the locomotives and insulated the leads. With the locomotives disabled the chance of another explosion was greatly diminished.

CHAPTER TWENTY THREE

In March, 1977, Scotia officials designated March 9 and 10 as Commemoration Days and declared that the mine would be closed on those two days. A memorial service was also scheduled to be held at the bathhouse to commemorate the dead miners. Reverend Bill Mackey of the Whitesburg First Baptist Church was scheduled to conduct the service.

When the area of the 2 Southeast Mains – Northeast Mains switch had been fully examined and explored and after the eleven bodies had been removed, Tommy Gross and I were tasked with bringing the two locomotives and two supply cars to the outside. I was in the front locomotive and Tommy was the operator of the rear one. Everything went smoothly all the way outside and up the slope but after we cleared the top of the rise on the main yard and stopped our train, Tommy jumped off his locomotive, gagging and nearly throwing up as he approached me. I asked him what was the matter and he replied, "The odor coming from the supply cars just about got me down. I tried to flag you to stop with my light but you must have not seen me. I'm still sick from breathing the odor!" I hadn't even thought about that possibility although we knew one of the dead miners had been found lying in one of the supply cars. I was thankful that I had chosen to operate the front locomotive when I heard Tommy's story.

When the necessary equipment had been moved to the new proposed section that I had helped to clean up, our second shift crew became a production crew of the first coal producing section since the explosions had disrupted production in the bottom mine. The new section, designated as 1 – West off South Mains Parallel, would be tasked to drive towards the 2 Southeast Mains section to provide a new air way to that part of the mine.

I started out on the section as the scoop operator but was approached by our boss one day who asked me if I would care to help our roof bolter operator instead. He said that no one could get along with the operator because he was so cranky and hateful. I asked the boss why he thought I might be able to better handle him and he told me that the bolter operator seemed to like me and maybe he would listen to me more than he would some of the other men. I then told the boss that I would try my hand at it but if I saw that I couldn't get along with him either, I wanted my job back. He agreed, so I became a reluctant roof bolter helper on a single head roof bolter.

Much to my surprise I found that the bolter operator and I got along fine, with no disagreements whatsoever. If I suggested something he listened to me and would usually see it my way because I was a stickler for safety and he knew I was only trying to look out for us both. I always watched the mine roof carefully when he or I was bolting and would warn him of any loose rock, as he would me also.

One thing he was deficient in was his safety practices when he was bolting a fresh cut of coal. He hardly ever drilled a test hole when going into a place to bolt it as he thought that it was a waste of time to drill an extra hole. I don't believe he understood that a test hole was drilled to see if there were any faults in the roof of the place to be bolted. For all we knew, there was a crack in the roof a few inches above the 5' bolts we were installing. If so, the bolts we were installing were useless and a roof fall was just waiting to happen. Without a test hole, we never knew for sure and it never became a habit for him to drill such a hole before installing roof bolts in the face despite my best efforts to convince him otherwise.

Drilling a test hole was part of our roof control plan and therefore was a requirement by law. Once, as we trammed our bolter into an entry where a fresh cut of coal had been taken out, I shook my light at him to stop. Stopping the bolter he hollered, "What's the matter?"

"Let's drill a test hole," I shouted over the loud roaring of the electric motor. He looked at me for a few seconds without replying and then just continued on into the fresh cut and began bolting, even before I got all my jacks set. I didn't like the fact that he ignored me, but I knew he would only say "I can't hear you", if I said anything more. He had done it before and played as if he was having trouble hearing me over the noise of the running roof bolter.

He had only drilled and tightened a couple of bolts when I saw Ray McKinney, a Federal Mine Inspector, round the corner of the break. Ray was a well-liked, very personable, and at the same time a strict, inspector who was smart and knew all the tricks of the trade when it came to coal mining. We had no idea he was even on the section. As soon as I saw his striped uniform coming into the entry I knew that as efficient as he was when inspecting a section that he would check for a test hole the first thing. I was right.

I saw him pulling out his tape measure and searching for the test hole as the bolt machine operator just kept drilling the hole he was working on. Ray walked up to the back of the bolting machine and I walked to meet him, He hollered, "Eddie, where's your test hole?" "We didn't drill one Ray." "Why not?" "I don't know, maybe he didn't hear me tell him to drill one, although I told him to." I'm pretty sure that Ray knew the situation as he knew both of us pretty well and had dealt with our section many times before.

He tapped the operator on the shoulder and turning around to face Ray, the operator shut the machine off. Ray then said, "Where's your test hole Sam?" I don't know, didn't you see it?" "No, Ray replied, I looked for it but it's not there." Sam then replied, "Well I guess I better back up and drill one then." "Good idea Sam, you do that." With that Sam backed up into the middle of the break and drilled his test hole. Lesson learned.

Sam once threatened another miner with a knife because the miner had jumped him verbally when Sam tore a check curtain down while trying to maneuver his bolting machine through the curtain. Both men were normally friends but it didn't take much to start a ruckus in an environment where the stress of constant danger surrounds you every second of every minute. Being over 1,400 feet beneath the surface of Big Black Mountain was in itself danger enough, much less fighting with your friends in a moment of anger and stress.

CHAPTER TWENTY FOUR

The deaths of the 26 men at killed Scotia in 1976 resulted in the passage of the Federal Mine Safety Act of 1977. This legislation strengthened provisions of the 1969 Act and also incorporated new mandates for all non-coal mines. The 1977 Act also renamed the Mine Safety and Enforcement Administration (MESA) as the Mine Safety and Health Administration., (MSHA), and moved the agency from the U.S. Department of the Interior to the U.S. Department of Labor.

1977 Public Law 95-164

Federal Mine Safety and Health Act of 1977

- Placed coal mines, metal and nonmetal mines under a single law, with enforcement provisions similar to 1969 Act. (Separate safety and health standards were retained.

- Moved enforcement agency to Department of Labor, renamed it Mine Safety and Health Administration, (MSHA)

- Requirement for four annual inspections at all underground mines, two at all surface mines.
- Advisory standards for metal and nonmetal mines eliminated.
- State enforcement plans in metal and nonmetal sector discontinued.
- Provisions for mandatory miner training.
- Mine rescue teams required for all underground mines.
- Increased involvement of miners and their representatives in health and safety activities.

This law should have been called, The Scotia Act, in my opinion, since the need for a rescue team immediately available was clearly shown by the events of March 9, and 11, 1976. Blue Diamond, to their credit, did embrace the idea and formed teams at their mines immediately after the twin explosions.

Another recent Act enacted by Congress was the:

Mine Improvement and New Emergency Response Act of 2006

This Act, (the MINER Act), was brought about by the explosion of the Sago mine in Upshur, Buckhannon

County, West Virginia, on January, 2, 2006, which killed 12 miners.

It stipulated that mine operators must provide caches of self-contained breathing apparatus along escape ways; the breathing apparatus must supply at least 2 hours of oxygen per miner and must be spaced no more than 30 minutes travel time apart to enable miners to make their way through the entire escapeway.

Before the Sago disaster, mine operators were only required to provide miners with a single self-contained breathing apparatus, providing one hour of oxygen. The only survivor of the group of Sago miners told rescuers that some miners thought their self-contained breathing apparatus was not working properly. Regulators felt miners needed to be provided with sufficient quantities of breathing apparatus to give them at least 2 hours of protection in the event of a prolonged escape. The MINER Act also calls for installation and maintenance of directional lifelines in escapeways.

In addition, the inability of trapped miners to communicate with rescuers during the Sago disaster led to another feature in the MINER Act. By July 2009, mine operators must install wireless two-way communications and tracking systems that will link surface rescuers with underground workers.

These Acts will provide needed protection for coal miners of the future, but too bad these laws weren't in effect before so many coal miners died to show the need for them.

In February, 1977, Scotia received a citation for violating water quality regulations. Scotia was sited after a Ky. State Bureau of Surface Mining Inspector visited the site of the sediment ponds located below the Scotia mine and near the Poor Fork of the Cumberland River.

The Inspector determined that the company was allowing too much coal sediment to enter the Cumberland River. The sediment included residue from coal-washing operations at the mine.

Cumberland, Kentucky city officials stated that the city had been having trouble cleaning the water that the city pumped from the river for its drinking water.

On several occasions in that month the city had to clean its water filters about three times as often per day because of the "black water" – believed to be coming from the Scotia mine ponds.

Scotia was ordered to clean out the ponds by the Bureau of Surface Mining Inspector and a second inspection showed that Scotia was taking steps to clean out the ponds and correct the problem. The Cumberland water supervisor stated a few weeks later that the river had been running clear for some time.

At some point in 1977, Scotia paid a fine of $25,000 dollars for water pollution. Whether the fine was for the above incident or another occurrence is not clear.

During the 1970's women began to enter the mining workforce. The first known woman coal miner to work in a U.S. coal mine started work in 1973. By 1980, of 255, 888 coal miners, 15,252 were women.

Scotia began hiring women miners in the 1970's also, and at first, only very few were seen inside the mine, but eventually several worked in coal production for Scotia through the remaining years of Scotia's operations. One woman was assigned to the section where I was a shuttle car operator and she was classified as a miner helper. She had no trouble at all with keeping the miner cable out of the way of the shuttle cars and continuous miner, and could handle the heavy loops of cable as well as any man.

A couple of times in the late 70's to the late 80's Scotia miners were picketed by the UMWA for reasons I don't remember at this late date. Their picket lines created a dilemma for us Scotia workers because we belonged to our own independent union who had not declared nor endorsed any strike. We were expected to work but at the same time we didn't want to cross a picket line set up by other fellow coal miners.

The first time we were picketed, we were still entering the bottom mine through the slope track entry and I believe the date was 1977. The bore hole had not yet been completed and the pickets were gathered at the main entrance beside Ky. 119 at the bridge.

The first day they showed up it seemed as though they were just milling around on the bridge and not trying to prevent anyone from entering Scotia property. I remember that I didn't realize that they were there to picket us because I saw no signs or any activity when I crossed the bridge. It was only when I got to the bathhouse to change into mining clothes and the Scotia workers were discussing the pickets that I realized we were being picketed.

I believe the UMWA miners were on strike at that time in reaction to cuts in their health benefits. Seven out of ten coal miners in Eastern Kentucky in that year were non-union workers, although some, including Scotia miners, were members of an independent union.

The pickets at Scotia's mine entrance were there again the next day when I came to work and this time they were in force. I decided to return home instead of having to try to break the line. I had personal days to take and I called one in so I wouldn't be docked any pay.

On the way home I came upon a large crowd of UMWA pickets standing in the entrance to South East Coal Company's Colson (Polly) mine. They were a much louder group than the one picketing our mine at Scotia and had numerous signs displayed. There seemed to be hundreds of them blocking access to the mine and I didn't see any miner crossing it at the time.

I lived just two miles from that mine and their operation was at least as large as Scotia's mine, if not larger. I began to believe that their strike might be a long one before it was over and I worried that night that our mine could be in for much trouble if the strike lasted a long time before any settlement might occur.

The next evening as I was going to Scotia for my regular shift I saw that the pickets at the South East mine were still there and that there seemed to be more of them than there were the day before. I dreaded to see how many we might have at Scotia when I got there. I had promised Wanda when leaving for work that day that I would return home and turn in another personal day if they were still at Scotia's entrance.

To my surprise, the pickets were gone when I arrived at work. I have no idea why they gave up but when talking to some of my co-workers I learned that most Scotia miners had crossed the UMWA picket line the day before without any major trouble breaking out. For some unexplained reason they had given up picketing.

The pickets at the South East mine near my home stayed on the line for several days and nights, and when going by there I never observed anyone crossing their picket line or trouble of any kind. I heard later that some of the miners had crossed the picket line eventually. After about a week they disappeared from South East's entrance and the workers returned to work in force.

In the 80's we were hit again with pickets from the UMWA, only this time we were entering the mine form the bore hole portal that had finally been finished. The bore hole, 376 feet deep and equipped with an elevator which would accommodate around 20 miners at a time to enter the mine. I don't remember the weight limits of the elevator but I believe 20 miners would have been under the limit.

This new mode of transportation allowed us to reach our coal producing sections much quicker than the slope entry and was in fact, many times safer than the steep slope. We were thankful to have it in operation. It was actually a little closer for me from my home also.

The UMWA pickets were blocking the road lead-ing to the bore hole one particular afternoon but moved to the side when I and other Scotia workers pulled up to where they were standing. I didn't understand who they were or why they were at first blocking the road, but I assumed they were UMWA miners, as I had read their contract was being negotiated at the time. I didn't under-stand why they let some of us through, but I was thank-ful that they did, and hoped their contract talks were set-tled soon.

It was not to be though and they returned day af-ter day for a few days in which some Scotia miners con-tinued to cross their picket line and some didn't. A few Scotia miners crossed the line even though the company never forced the issue with our workers, who mostly just didn't show up for work while the pickets were there.

I know of at least one, a Scotia foreman, who sped through the line one day and ended up with four flat tires on his truck. I had heard of that tactic before which had been used to assure that no one crossed the line, using a gadget called "jack nails." which were 2" nails welded in-to the shape of children's toy jacks. Other Scotia miners were said to have been a victim also. Fortunately the strike ended up being settled fairly quickly and things were soon back to normal.

The UMWA weren't the only miners who would strike for a better contract. The 1985 contract talks between the Scotia Employees Union and Scotia hit a snag in February, 1985, when the company put forth a proposal for workers to accept a 10 hours per day, 4 days a week work schedule. To sweeten the pot they also offered a $100.00 signing bonus when the contract was approved and signed. The following letter was sent to Scotia Employee Association members:

Notice
Special Called Meeting

There will be a "Special Called Meeting" Saturday, March 2, 1985 at 9 a.m. at the union hall.

The primary purpose of the meeting is to <u>discuss</u> the proposed 4 day work week offered by the company.

At the Union meeting of Feb. 16, 1985 the Executive Board of the Union was requested, by majority vote: to approach the Company for a written copy of their proposal and if they felt their proposal had merit, each member was to be sent a copy, and a "Special Meeting" was to be called, to vote on whether to "enter into contract negotiations at this time."

The Executive Board has voted unanimously to veto this proposal, as authorized at the last meeting. We do, however, feel that each member should be informed as to the contents of the proposal.

The matter concerning whether or not we want to enter into negotiations at this time, for a new short contract, until July, needs to be finalized at this meeting.

Each member of the Union should make every effort to attend this meeting, as decisions made in the Union Hall are binding on the Union Membership as a whole.

Mike Dingus, Sec. / Treas.
(Signed Mike Dingus)

As negotiations continued, it was agreed by both the Company and Scotia Employees Association (SEA), that the contract signed in July, 1982 would continue to be in force and negotiations between the two parties would continue until a settlement could be agreed on.

CHAPTER TWENTY FIVE

On November 20, 1985, a supplemental agreement was signed into effect by the SEA and Company officials. The amended contract is as follows:

Final Company Offer
SCOTIA EMPLOYEES ASSOCIATION
November 20, 1985

Article II- Recognition

Amend Section 1 to include Middle Taggart.

Amend the first literary paragraph of section 2 to read as follows:

Section 2. This agreement shall not cover coal inspectors or weight bosses at mines where men are paid by the ton: watchmen, clerks, engineering or technical forces of the operator, working at or from district or local mine offices: independent contractors or lessees engaged in coal or non-coal producing activities pursuant to contract or lease with the Operator, unless such contractors or lessees or their employees mine coal through the portals in any underground mine which was being operated by the operator within its leasehold at Scotia on April 30, 1982.

Article III- Management Rights

Amend Section 3, to read as follows:

At the Scotia Plant or Train Loader, the Company shall not purchase or process any outside or leased coal while any of the workforce is laid off. This shall not include coal produced at the Royal Diamond Mine.

Article VI- Wages and Hours

Amend Section 7, Repairmen pay as follows:

Repairmen pay: Repairmen shall receive first class repairmen wages when, in the opinion of Management, such repairmen are qualified (including all required State and Federal Certificates). Beltmen shall receive Belt Repairmen wages when, in the opinion of Management such beltmen are qualified. Any future Belt Repairmen or Pumpers shall be required to obtain all required Stare and Federal Certificates in order to be qualified.

Amend Section 8 to provide for an increase in wages over and above the rate of pay presently being paid as follows:

12/1/85   12/1/86   12/1/87

$4.00 per man per day $5.00 per day $6.00 per day

255

Article VII- Payday

Amend the third paragraph to read as follows:

Payments shall be made in cash or check, with recognition for legitimate deductions. Statement of earnings and current deductions in detail shall be issued to employees. Year-to-date figures on accumulated earnings, Federal Income Tax withheld, F.I.C.A. withheld, State Income Tax withheld, hours worked and foreman number shall also be shown. The Company will be given appropriate time to reprogram its computer.

Article VIII- Hospitalization and Insurance Benefits

Amend as follows:

Section 1. The operator shall provide hospitalization, medical, dental, and drug benefits as presently being provided for active employees.

Delete Section 3 in its entirety and add a new section to read as follows:

The Company will provide the same level of medical benefits to pensioners who have retired prior to December 1, 1985, that have been provided in the past.

Delete Section 5- ($5,000.00 lump sum paid by Company.)

Amend Section 6 by increasing the amount of group life insurance from $10,000.00 to $25,000.00 double indemnity.

Add new Section- to read as follows:

It is agreed that the operator will pay in-hospital sick pay to any Employee with one (1) year's continuous record of employment, who is hospitalized for illness or injury other than alcoholism, drug addiction, or injuries covered by workmen's Compensation, during their hospitalization period not to exceed five (5) work days per year at their regular rate of pay.

Article IX- Pension Benefits

Amend Section 3 as follows:

Increase benefits from $18.00 per month per year of benefit service to:

A. 1/1/86	1/1/87	1/1/88
$23.00 per month-	$24.00	$25.00
Per year benefit service	"	"

C. $250.00 minimum retirement benefits.

Article XI- Vacation Pay

Amend the first literary paragraph of Section 1 as follows:

The following annual vacation periods are established:

The first week of vacation to be taken during that week which includes the 4th of July and a second week of vacation to commence on December 24th, through January 1st. Men required to work during these periods at operations which are necessarily continuous or on emergencies or repair work, may have vacation of the same duration at other agreed periods. All employees who are on the payroll for the entire periods between semi-annual vacations, shall receive Six Hundred ($600.00) Dollars at each semi-annual vacation for the second contract year, and Six Hundred ($600.00) Dollars for the third contract year.

Add three (3) additional extra vacation days for a total of ten (10) days one through ten years.

Article XII- Seniority & Opportunity

Delete this article in its entirety and add a new article to read as follows:

Section 1. Seniority in principle and practice shall be recognized in the operator's mines commencing with the date when each employee began work.

Section 2. The management of the mine shall have the direction of the working force. Preference in the shift seniority will be given to those persons with the most seniority at the mine providing it does not disrupt the operation of the mine insofar as mine management is concerned.

Section 3. The procedure for filling vacancies shall be as follows:

a.   Should a vacancy occur on the first or second shift, such vacancy shall be filled by the person in that classification with the most seniority from either the second or third shift.

b.   The vacancy remaining after implementing shift seniority shall be filled by the employee with the most mine seniority who has been reclassified due to a reduction in the working force, provided he signified in writing prior to the occurrence of a vacancy that he desires to return to the classification that he was in at the time of the cut-off. An employee may withdraw his election to return to his former classification without penalty prior to a vacancy occurring in that classification.

c.   The vacancy created by the employee being transferred to his former classification shall be filled by the person in that classification with the most mine seniority from either the second or third shift.

d.   In the event of a vacancy in a job classification on the first or second shift, that is not filled in accordance with paragraph (a), (b), and (c), the company shall post a notice on the bulletin board. Any qualified employee desiring to advance to another job classification shall have three days in which to submit a bid in person to a designated representative of the company, and the company shall fill the vacancy with the senior qualified employee. Employees thus placed in a new classification shall be given not more than thirty (30) days to prove their ability.

e.   Any vacancy remaining after (a), (b). (c), and (d) above have been implemented shall be filled by the senior qualified employee on the idle panel. If more than one vacancy is to be filled, the senior qualified employee on the idle panel shall be given the vacancy of his preference.

f.   Any employee choosing a new classification and proving incapable of handling the position shall be subject to discharge at the option of the Company. Among the reasons to deem an employee incapable of handling such position shall be creating a hazard to the employees safety, the handling of equipment in a manner destructive to the equipment, and the in ability to maintain a satisfactory level of productivity.

g.   In the event no qualified employee bids for the vacancy or can be returned from the panel, the Company may hire a qualified person from those seeking employment.

h.   Should there be no suitable person available within the work force or job applications, and a person must be trained, the Company will post a notice of such vacancy on the bulletin boards. Any employee desiring to advance to another job classification or outside job shall have three (3) days in which to bid in person to a designated representative of the Company, and the Company shall fill the vacancy with the senior person. Any underground vacancies created by said bid shall be filled at the discretion of the Company, except all outside vacancies shall be posted.

i.   No employee shall change classifications as hereinabove provided more than once every year.

Section 4. In all cases where the working force is to be reduced, employees in each job classification at the mines with the least total service at the mines shall be laid off first, however, in the event any employee who has more seniority is to be cut off and put on a panel, mine management shall offer such employee a job in another classification for which he is qualified, and shall, if accepted by such employee, cut off the man having the least seniority in this classification.

Section 5. Employees who are idle because of a reduction in the working force shall be placed in a panel from which they shall be returned to employment based on the basis of seniority. When an employee is to be called back from the panel the Company will contact him by telephone. If this cannot be accomplished, a registered letter will be sent to his last known address and the employee will be required to, immediately upon receiving this letter, notify the Company of his intention to return to work.

Section 6. Any idle employee may be re-employed in a new classification, providing such person is qualified for the job and is entitled to the job by reason of his seniority.

Section 7. The superintendent of the mine and the secretary of the Union shall be joint custodians of the panel record.

Section 8. Any person on the panel list who secures casual or intermittent employment during the period when no work is available for him at the operation shall in no way jeopardize his seniority rights while engaged in such temporary employment. However, any person on the panel who secures regular employment at another operation, or outside the industry, and does not return to work when there is available employment at the mine for those in said panel, shall sacrifice his seniority rights to the operation and shall have his name removed from the panel list.

Section 9. All new employees shall be considered probationary employees for the first thirty (30) calendar days of their employment. The employer may terminate their employment within such period without cause or other justifications.

Section 10. Grievances under the provisions of this Article XII shall be handled in the usual way under the machinery of the contract providing for the consideration and disposition of grievances.

Section 11. In carrying out the provision of this Article XII, management shall be the sole judge of "Qualifications" of the employee or applicant.

Article XIII- Union Officials

Delete the words mine committee wherever they are used in the contract and replace the words Union Officials. These Union officials shall be limited to six (6) in number at any one time.

Article XVIII- MISCELLANEOUS PROVISIONS

Any graduated vacation days and personal days to which an Employee called back from the panel might be entitled for each category shall be reduced to the following percentages rounded to the nearest whole day:

Time remaining to be worked in contract year

9 months to less than one year 100%

6 months to 9 months........................75%

3 months to 6 months....................50%

Less than 3 months........................25%

Due to the fact that the period from July 15 through November 30 was worked under the terms of the old contract, employees shall receive credit for a pro-rata share of personal days and graduated vacation days from the old contract in addition to the days specified in the new contract, less any days taken during the period July 15 through November 30, 1985. Accordingly, a schedule of days off for the first year of the contract is attached hereto as exhibit "D'

Section 10- Bereavement pay to read as follows:

A maximum of three (3) days bereavement pay as a result of the death of employee's spouse, mother, father, brother, sister, daughter, son, mother-in-law, father-in-law- or grandparents. These three days shall be paid at straight time rates and shall be three consecutive days, one of which shall be the day of the funeral. Any regular scheduled working day falling within these three days shall be an excused absence.

Add Section to read as follows:

$400.00 per man signing bonus to be paid as soon as possible after the contract has been signed.

Article XX- Effective Date

Amend as follows:

This contract dated this ....day of November, 1985, shall be and become effective from and after the 1st day of December, 1985, and shall continue in effect for a period of three (3) years from and after said date, and thereafter unless cancelled by either party upon sixty (60) days of written notice.

Successor Clause:

This Contract shall be binding upon the Company, its Successors, and Assigns.

Exhibit "D"

Personal Days and Graduated Vacation Days for the Contract Beginning December 1, 1985 through November 10, 1986

Employees shall receive during the first contract year personal days and graduated vacation days according to the schedule herein below, less any personal days and graduated vacation days taken during the period July 15 through November 30, 1985.

Personal days – 4

Graduated Vacation Days:

Years Service	Days Off
0-1	1
1-2	3

Years Service	Days Off
2-3	4
3-4	6
4-5	7
5-6	8
6-7	10

7-8	11
8-9	12
9-10	14
10-11	15

The schedule herein above shall apply only to the first contract year and beginning in the second year, the personal days and graduated vacation days shall be taken in accordance with the terms of the new contract.

The Nov. 20th contract amendments listed above required some contentious negotiating before they were agreed to by all parties concerned. Scotia Union employees spent a few days on the picket line before serious talks got underway.

We set up our picket line at the Frank's Creek borehole entrance and no Scotia employees worked producing coal for about 4 or 5 days while we were striking. Several picket posts were set up along the dirt road and S.E.A. Union members were assigned certain hours to be on the picket line on the same shift they worked in the mine.

The lines were manned 24 hours a day and during that time we never had to deal with any strike breakers or by having anyone trying to break the line. Actually the

Union members and management got along just fine during the strike and when the foremen and supervisors drove up to the line at the beginning of a shift, they were waved on through by the miners. After all, we wanted to make sure the mine was firebossed, the water pumped, and the equipment kept in good shape for when we returned to work, (as we knew we eventually would.)

When the Company offered to work under the old contract and continue negotiations we went back to work. The amended contract was finally agreed to and endorsed by both parties. We also agreed to the 4 day-10 hours per day schedule at that time.

CHAPTER TWENTY SIX

In 1978, Blue Diamond Coal Company made a tentative agreement to sell all their coal mining assets to Standard Oil of Indiana. Under terms of the agreement Indiana Standard would exchange 2.6 million of its common shares for the six coal mines Scotia owned in Kentucky, Tennessee, and Virginia.

Blue Diamond's coal mines produced slightly less than 2 million tons of coal in 1977 and their coal revenue for the whole year was estimated at about 46 million dollars. Blue Diamond's Justus mine located in Stearns, Kentucky had been the focus of organizing efforts by the UMWA for over three years at that time and had reportedly been the scene of gunfire and other violence.

In 1979 Blue Diamond filed a $100 million suit against Blackwood Land Company, the owner of the coal Scotia was mining, which the Knoxville based corporation was leasing. Blue Diamond claimed that Blackwood intentionally interfered with a proposal last fall to sell all the coal assets to Standard Oil of Indiana by casting a cloud upon the title of the coal lease at the Scotia Mines. Regardless of the reason, the sale never went through and Scotia continued to produce coal under the Blue Diamond banner. Most Scotia miners, me included, were not aware that Scotia was negotiating a sale at that time.

At one point after the bottom mine was reopened, my fresh air crew buddies and I were sent to a new opening in the Imboden mine that was driving new entries for ventilation improvement. The mine was located on the dirt road that led from the guard shack to the Scotia mining complex.

I don't know who gave that mine the moniker of "Slick Rock" but the name was very appropriate. The opening was one entry only and was a slope opening, being nearly straight down for several breaks and slick as a ribbon and nearly impossible to walk down without nearly falling several times in the process, Water and mud ran down the slope of the mine constantly and gathered at the bottom in pools that had to be constantly pumped outside the mine to try to control.

Cold and miserable would not begin to describe the conditions we encountered and endured at Slick Rock during the winter. Even walking down the slick and muddy slope was almost impossible without losing your footing and falls were frequent and resulted in a few minor injuries. We finally solved the problem by using the bucket of our scoop as a mantrip to transport the men into and out of the mine.

The scoop was also used as our supply transport vehicle and timber hauler. We were using 8 foot long and 8"square creosote timbers to support the roof at Slick Rock because the roof conditions were so poor. The conditions were so bad on the steep entry that a very small tracked dozer-like vehicle with forks attached was brought in to help with loading and transporting the heavy timbers inside the mine. The scoop became useless after a while and the small dozer was very adept at crawling up and down the steep slope and very muddy roadway so we used it extensively instead of the scoop.

We were working close enough to the outside that we could eat our lunches outside when the weather permitted while at Slick Rock. One incident that occurred one day nearly resulted in a clash between two of our fellow miners. When one miner opened his dinner bucket, he looked at the sandwich his wife had prepared for him, and with an oath he took the sandwich from his bucket and without looking, flung it directly into the side of another miner's face. The miner he hit was unaware as to why he had been slapped with a sandwich, and thought it had been done on purpose. With an oath he jumped up and was ready to jump the sandwich thrower, who quickly and vehemently apologized and affirmed to his fellow miner that he hadn't meant to hit him, that it had been an accident.

Both miners were known to be quick-tempered but were normally friends, so both eventually traded apologies over the situation. Sadly, both are now deceased as are so many of our friends and co-workers of that time.

On March 8, 1978, nearly two years to the day since the twin explosions occurred in the Scotia mine, Federal mine officials served Scotia Coal Company with 44 notices of mine violations and 28 closure orders stemming from the two explosions of March 9, and 11, 1976.

The citations and closure orders, most of them for federal mine law violations which had since been corrected, resulted from the investigation of the Scotia disaster made by the Mining Enforcement and Safety Administration, (MESA). The orders and notices were served on Scotia even though the report on the investigation was still under wraps at that date.

Details of the orders and notices were not immediately available but officials said that the MESA investigation showed electrical violations resulting in 14 closure orders and 11 citations; ventilation violations resulting in 12 closure orders and 10 citations; and explosives violations leading to 13 citations. The investigation had covered the entire mine, according to officials.

At the time of the investigations one section only was in production, (1 – West off South Mains, the new airway section where I was a shuttle car operator) and most of the activity was centered around construction of new airways and escapeways.

The investigation had lasted six months, during which no new evidence relating to the explosions of March, 1976 had been found. The violations found during the investigation included five different violations of "firebossing" violations. According to testimony at the Department of Interior hearings, Scotia officials failed to make required pre-shift examinations for methane accumulations in many sections of the mine.

Scotia also failed to report a methane ignition in December, 1975, failed to provide adequate firefighting and escape training, and allowed miners to go underground without training in the use of self-rescuers. The 25 electrical regulation violations also included a citation on the locomotive which was suspected to have touched off the first explosion.

By January, 1979 Scotia had three sections in the bottom mine, two were sections tasked specifically for coal production, and the new airway section (1 West) which was not configured for high production of coal but was instead driving towards the 2 Southeast Mains section where the first explosion (and probably the second also) occurred. The plan was to drive the airway to within 200 feet of the 2 Southeast Mains section and stop while plans were made for entering the potentially explosive section. Once 2 Southeast Mains was driven into, the entire Scotia mine would be ventilated and accessible for the first time since the explosions occurred.

One Mining, Health, and Safety Administration official commented in the month of March, 1979, that, *"It's logical to assume that there is a lot of methane in there,* (Southeast Mains). *That is probably to our advantage since anything over 15 percent is not explosive,"* he said. *"We hope the methane level is around 70 to 80 percent."*

Samples taken from behind the seals at that time in Southeast Mains averaged 12-13 percent methane at #1 seal and 1-2 percent at number 8 seal. The low methane levels were attributed to the absence of coal production in the section.

While working at Slick Rock doing timber work, we sometimes found ourselves sidetracked by being assigned another job at another location on the Scotia supply yard or in another area of Scotia property. One evening we were sent to the belt line drift mouth of the bottom mine to do some such job that I don't remember now but I do remember an alarming incident (to me) while we were working there. For some reason the need for an end loader operator came up to help in our outside work. I had some experience in operating the big 988 Hough loader on the supply yard but was still not experienced enough to say that I was proficient on it.

The boss was aware that I had operated the loader occasionally, so when the need for the loader came up while at the outside belt entry that day, he asked me to fetch the 988 and bring it across a narrow bridge near the belt entry. It was nearly dark when I drove to our work site. When I approached the bridge a co-worker watched my wide tires to make sure I had enough rubber on the bridge to avoid toppling into the gully under the bridge. With him watching I drove across the bridge and did whatever the job was that the loader was required to do. After finishing the job, the boss instructed me to take the loader onto the coal stockpile at the tipple where it was needed to push coal with. My buddy that had watched me across the bridge earlier again performed the same chore as I went back across it.

After I had driven the 988 Hough onto the stockpile and turned it over to another miner who was to push the coal, I walked back to the belt entry where my crew was working and asked the man who had watched me as I drove across the bridge how much tire I had to spare on the loader while crossing the bridge. He grinned and said, "Buddy, you had an inch of tire on one side and two inches on the other!" My knees went weak when I learned how close I had come to flipping the loader into the 10' foot gully when crossing that bridge that night. Some of the men later complimented me on my expertise when bringing the loader across the bridge. I told them that expertise had nothing to do with it, but that blissful ignorance and stupidity had a lot to do with it.

CHAPTER TWENTY SEVEN

The following incident occurred in one of Scotia's Upper Taggart mines in April, 1976, just after the two explosions in the Scotia #1 mine. The upper mines went back to work in the latter part of March after a week off in memory of the 26 fallen miners. Naturally, and especially after what happened in Scotia's bottom mine. MESA inspectors were quick to inspect the Upper Taggart mines as soon as they returned to work. This report involves a violation found in the One Right section of the mine. A hearing on the violation was held in 1978 concerning the violation which Scotia trying to overturn. Scotia wanted the penalty for the violation dismissed, thus the hearing was held concerning the violation in front of an Administrative Law Judge.

The citation was for a violation of 30 CFR 75.1725 – <u>Machinery and Equipment operation and maintenance</u>.

Issues

The issues raised by the petition for Assessment of Civil Penalty are whether a violation of section 75.1725 occurred and, if so, what civil penalty should be assessed, based on the six criteria set forth in section 110 (1 of the Act.

Findings of Fact

1. Ronald E. Suttles, a Federal coal mine inspector, was in the process of making a complete inspection of respondent's Upper Taggart Mine when he received a complaint regarding a shuttle car in the one right section of respondent's mine. Inspector Suttles went to the one right section on Monday, April 19, 1976, to determine whether there was any validity to the complaint. The inspector asked Joe Pratt, the operator of the B-29 shuttle car, to maneuver the car so that inspector Suttles could determine whether it was in safe operating condition. Inspector Suttles concluded that the wheels on one side of the shuttle car would not turn properly. He considered that the shuttle car created a hazard to any miners near the car because the shuttle car had to be backed up several times when the operator of the car needed to receive

coal from the continuous mining machine, go around corners, or dump coal at the belt feeder.

2. Despite the fact that the B29 car was not in safe operating condition on April 19, 1976, Inspector Shuttles did not write a notice of violation or order of withdrawal with respect to the unsafe car. Inspector Suttles stated that new management had just taken over the operation of the Upper Taggart Mine. The inspector had been getting good cooperation from the new management and accepted management's assurances that the car would be fixed without the necessity of the inspector's writing an order or notice of violation with respect to the car.

3. Inspector Suttles stated that when he returned to the mine on April 20, 1976, he saw the B29 shuttle car being operated. Inspector Suttles was "pretty sure" that the same operator, Joe Pratt, was driving the shuttle car. Mr. Pratt told Inspector Suttles that the car had not been repaired. Inspector Suttles then issued at 9:55 a.m. unwarrantable failure order No. 2 RDS under section 104 (C) (2) of the Federal Coal Mine Health and Safety Act of 1969. Order No. 2 RDS cited respondent for a violation of section 75. 1725 because the B 29 shuttle car (6SC) being used in the One Right Section was not being main-

tained in a safe operating condition in that the steering was bad and the operator could not safely steer the car through crosscuts. Section 75.1725 requires mobile equipment to be maintained in safe operating condition, or requires, in the alternative, that unsafe equipment be removed from service immediately.

4. James Bentley, respondent's safety inspector, testified that when he and Inspector Suttles came to the face area of the One Right Section on April 20, 1976, the miners were in the process of opening a new section of the mine off the old section in which they had been working. Mr. Bentley said the B 29 car had been repaired on the 11 p.m. – 7 a.m. shift on April 20 and that the car had not been moved on the day shift of April 20 because there was not sufficient room between the place where the belt feeder was located and the working face for two shuttle cars to be operated. Mr. Bentley said that new parts had been installed on the B 29 shuttle car and that the old parts were still lying beside the car. The old parts had to be picked up so that the car could be moved. Mr. Bentley said that the operator of the B 29 car got up on it and moved it a few feet but that there was not enough room for it to be operated very much.

5. Timothy Maggard, a repairman who normally works on the 3 p.m. to 11 p.m. shift, testified that the B29 car broke down on his shift on April 19, 1976, at about 8:30 p.m. Mr. Maggard made a temporary repair of the B 29 car on April 19 so that the car could be used up to the end of the production shift which ended at 11:00 p.m. Mr. Maggard said that the steering mechanism on the B 29 car was so bad that he decided that it needed to be completely rebuilt. Although Mr. Maggard had already worked his full 8 hour shift by 11:00 p.m., he continued to work overtime on the next shift (11 p.m. to 7 a.m.) so that the B 29 car would be in good operating condition for the beginning of the next production shift which was due to start at 7 a.m. Mr. Maggard had completed the repair of the B 29 car by 5 a.m. on April 20. He was due to report back to the mine to work his regular shift which began at 3 p.m. that same day. Therefore, Mr. Maggard obtained the promise of the other repairmen on the 11 p.m. to 7 a.m. shift that they would take the old parts to the end of the track for him and he went home to get some sleep before reporting back to the mine at 3 p.m. Before Mr. Maggard left for home, however, he drove the B 29 car around the block in each direction to make sure that all wheels were turning properly when the machine was maneuvered around corners.

280

6. When Mr. Maggard returned to the mine to work his regular shift commencing at 3 p.m. on April 20, 1976, he found that a red tag had been placed on the B 29 car indicating that the car was the subject of a withdrawal order. Mr. Maggard first checked the car's steering by jacking it up. He turned the car's steering wheel in one direction and checked the wheels on both sides of the car to make certain that they turned. He then turned the steering wheel in the opposite direction and found that the wheels all turned properly in that direction also. Mr. Maggard thereafter drove the car around the block and could find nothing wrong with it. Therefore he parked the car where he found it with the red tag still on it. He then reported to the maintenance foreman that he could find nothing with the B 29 car. When Mr. Maggard reported for work on his regular shift on April 21, 1976, he found that the red tag had been removed from the B 29 car and that it was being used.

7. Richard Combs, who was general mine foreman at the Upper Taggart Mine on April 19 and 20, 1976, testified that the time sheets in the company's files show that Mr. Maggard worked a regular 8 hour shift on April 19 and worked 8 hours of overtime on the 11 p.m. to 7 a.m. shift on April 20.

8. In his rebuttal testimony, Inspector Suttles first stated that there was more room for use of the B 29 car on April 20, 1976, than the company's witnesses had described. Inspector Suttles conceded, however, that his memory of the conditions in the One Right Section on April 20 was not distinct and that the continuous mining machine might have been involved in cleaning up the mine floor for commencement of mining operations in a different direction. If that were true, respondent's claim that there was insufficient room for operation of two shuttle cars was probably correct. Inspector Suttles stated that he was not entirely certain about what the miners were doing on the 20th, but he was certain that there was sufficient space for both shuttle cars to be used on the 21st.

Nonoccurrence of Violation

I find that the preponderance of the evidence supports a conclusion that no violation of section 75.1725 occurred on April 20, 1976. There is no doubt but that the steering on the B 29 shuttle car was defective on April 19, 1976, as both Inspector Shuttles and the repairman, Mr. Maggard, agreed that the steering on the B 29 shuttle car was in bad condition on April 19, 1976, when Inspector Suttles asked that it be repaired. If Inspector Suttles had cited the B 29 shuttle car for a violation of section 75. 1725 on April 19, 1976, there is no reason to believe that respondent's management would have contested the violation.

If the inspector had been more certain of what he actually saw on April 20 when he came back to check the condition of the B 29 car, it is possible that I could have found in his favor, but his admission that he could not recall for certain what the miners were doing on the 20th, as opposed to the 21st, makes it impossible to find in his favor. Mr. Maggard's demeanor at the hearing was that of a truthful witness and his testimony is consistent throughout. Both his direct testimony and his cross-examination show that he specifically recalled the rebuilding of the steering system on the B 29 shuttle car. The fact that he personally drove the car after it was repaired is a very convincing reason to believe that he had satisfactorily repaired the B 29 shuttle car before Inspector Suttles ever issued Order No. 2 RDS citing the car for a violation of section 75. 1725. Additionally, Mr. Maggard jacked up the car to test the steering on the 20th after the order was issued without finding anything wrong with it. The fact that nothing was done to the B 29 car between the time the inspector issued his order and the next day when it was found to be in proper operating condition, is strong and convincing evidence that nothing was wrong with the steering on the B 29 car at the time the inspector's order was written.

At transcript page 41 Mr. Bentley referred to the fact that both the inspector and respondent's management were under a lot of pressure at the time the inspector issued his order on April 20, 1976. As I have indicated in finding No. 1, supra, Inspector Suttles had received a complaint to the effect that the B 29 shuttle car was being operated in an unsafe condition. Even though he found that the B 29 shuttle car was unsafe on April 19, the inspector did not write an order or notice citing management for the violation at the time the violation was observed. It appears that the inspector's failure to cite a violation on the 19th may have been the subject of criticism. Therefore, when he returned to the mine on April 20th, he was under pressure to cite the company for the violation which did exist the previous day but which did not exist on April 20 when he actually wrote his order of withdrawal.

The inspector's order is dated April 20, 1976, so there is no question before me as to whether the inspector could have backdated his order to cite respondent on the 20th for a violation which he observed on the 19th. The finding of a violation can be sustained only if the testimony shows that the B 29 shuttle car was defective on the 20th. The preponderance of the evidence shows that the car had been repaired between 11 p.m. on the 19th and the time that the inspector saw the car on the 20th.Since the car was not in an unsafe condition on the 20th, no violation of section 75.1727 existed when Order No. 2 RDB was written.

Ultimate Findings and Conclusions

(1) The petition for Assessment of Civil Penalty filer in Docket No. BARB 78-401-P should be dismissed because of MSHA's failure to prove that a violation of section 75.1725 occurred as alleged in Order No. 2 RDS (6-206 dated April 20, 1976.)

(2) Scotia Coal Company was the operator of the Upper Taggart Mine at all pertinent times and as such is the subject to the provisions of the Act and to the health and safety standards promulgated thereunder.

WHEREFORE, it is ordered:

The petition for Assessment of Civil Penalty filed May 12, 1978, in Docket No. BARB 78-401-P is dismissed for the reason stated in paragraph (1) above.

Richard C. Steffey
Administrative Law Judge

This ruling was in Scotia's favor, which was needed for morale purposes if for nothing else. The judge was right about the integrity of Timothy Maggard. He was one of the finest people I ever worked with and was as honest as could be found in a person. I first worked with him in 1964 when we were both employed at a garage in Whitesburg and he was one of the more skilled mechanics working there.

CHAPTER TWENTY EIGHT

In 1979, Blue Diamond Coal Company filed a $100 million dollar suit against Blackwood Land Company, the owner of much of the coal properties near Eolia, Kentucky. Blue Diamond claimed that Blackwood intentionally interfered with a proposal to sell all its coal assets to Standard oil of Indiana by casting a cloud upon the title of the lease at Scotia.

In the early part of that year, MHSA officials were calling the Scotia mine "one of the safest mines in Letcher County." M.H.S.A.'s Whitesburg office attributed the safe conditions to two factors; increased inspection by their office and rehabilitation efforts undertaken by the company since the March, 1976 disaster.

Two MSHA inspectors, one on each production shift, were then inspecting Scotia's (#1 mine) each day as part of the federal inspectors program. This program placed federal mine inspectors full time in mines with a history of safety problems.

The supervisor of MESA's Whitesburg office said at the time that his inspector's responsibilities include frequent checks for excessive methane gas and inadequate ventilation. *"The mine is monitored very closely than any other mine in Letcher County,*" the supervisor reported.

While the rehabilitation of Scotia's #1 mine was in progress, another tragic event was taking place in one of Scotia's Upper Taggart mines. On March 14, 1979, a roof fall accident killed two Scotia miners and injured a third miner. The two men killed were section foreman Grant Sturgill, age 45, of Partridge, Kentucky, and section utility man Ernest Stetzer, 38, of Eolia, Kentucky. The men were pillaring out of the section when the roof collapsed. Continuous miner operator Larkin Napier, age 30, was injured and was trapped by the fall for nearly six hours until rescuers could free him.

Pillaring coal is a method of mining coal that involves the removing the large blocks of coal (pillars) that support the roof when mining advances into the coal. As each pillow is removed, the roof under the pillar collapses, allowing the roof to cave in, which relieves the pressure on the roof behind the retreating miners and mining equipment.

The resulting falls are intentional and this method of mining is probably one of the most dangerous methods of mining underground, but unfortunately accidents do occur even when the mining of pillars is done according to plan.

I was a shuttle car operator on several pillaring sections in the Scotia (#1) bottom mine in the 1980"s and I always observed that miners appear to mine more safely when pillaring and are much more watchful and aware of the roof conditions than when advance mining. My observation of those doing this type of mining is that they have much more awareness of what's going on around them and are quick to warn fellow miners of any dangerous conditions, especially roof conditions.

One experienced miner that seemed to have a knack for sensing when the roof in a pillaring section was in danger of an imminent fall was Clifford Smith, who was the continuous miner operator in several pillaring sections I worked on. Many times when Clifford was loading my shuttle car with coal he would stop the loading and shake his cap light vigorously at me to "get out of the way," so he could back the miner out of the cut. It usually took only a few minutes before a large roof fall occurred, relieving the pressure on the section. I always felt secure when pillaring because I knew he was observing the roof conditions even as he cut the coal and would warn us car drivers of when danger loomed with the roof. Of course even with the most experienced miners, pillaring was still the most dangerous type of mining coal that I experienced and almost cost my section a continuous mining machine once.

This happened when I was operating my shuttle car while pillaring and was under the boom of the miner with my car receiving a load of coal. Clifford all at once stopped the conveyor of the mining machine and as he backed out I saw he was intently watching the roof as he trammed the miner backwards. The miner helper was frantically putting loops of cable onto the hooks located on the side of the miner as I was hurriedly backing my shuttle car out of the entry.

When the miner had nearly reached the last row of resin bolts of the cut, the roof caved in with a crash and a large boom which reverberated throughout the section. The rock and coal dust blocked my view for a few seconds and I first thought that the miner had been covered up by the fall and while Clifford was still in the deck of the miner. When the dust cleared, I saw the miner helper's light and knew he was O.K. and then saw that Clifford was out of the miner's deck and they were both hurrying towards the entry where my car was located.

It was a close call that day, but everyone escaped without injury, except for bruised egos. The continuous mining machine was trapped under the rock from just in front of the operator's deck to, and including the heads of the miner. It seemed a hopeless case at first glance of ever being able to recover the mining machine.

As the rest of the section's crew gathered around, the fear of more rock falling kept any effort of trying to remove the machine out from under the pile of rock. It was best to wait a while to see if another fall might occur.

Eventually, after about an hour, it was decided to attach a ¾ inch steel rope to the miner boom and attach the end of the cable to my shuttle car and try to pull the miner out from beneath the rock. The other car driver also attached a steel rope from his car to mine to provide double pulling power. The miner operator was to help by starting the machine and at the same time we pulled, to try to tram the miner out from under the rock.

We started our cars and even with Clifford holding the tram levers down, we couldn't budge the miner. Nothing we did would move it one inch. We gave it a try several times but had to eventually give up the effort as useless as teats on a boar hog.

I climbed on the top of the miner boom to use a wrench to take the clamp off the steel rope so I could remove the shuttle car from the entry in case another fall should occur, since it was then near quitting time for our crew. This was a mistake.

While hunkered down to remove the clamp, the roof again started cracking and popping with pieces of drawrock falling on top of the rock which had fallen in the first incident. Without a second thought, I leaped from the miner boom to the ground, landing on some large rocks that had fallen there when the first fall occurred. I then scurried to the crosscut of the entry we were in, and then realized that I had injured my foot in the jump.

While I examined my foot, our foreman decided that no other measures would be taken in trying to pull the miner free from the rock until the roof settled down. Our shift was nearly at an end anyway and we knew other measures would be necessary to free the mining machine, if it could be retrieved at all.

After arriving outside I was barely able to walk to the car to go home and didn't even attempt to take a shower, but went straight to the hospital E.R to have the foot X-rayed. According to the technician, there was no break, but the foot was just badly bruised. The next morning, I went to see my family physician, who then examined my foot, and agreed with the original diagnosis. He said that I would have to take at least a month off from work to allow the very badly sprained and bruised foot to heal.

I didn't argue with him, as I couldn't even wear a shoe or boot that day because of the swelling. I went back every week for follow-up visits and had another X-ray which confirmed there was no break in the foot, but I personally thought the break had "missed a good chance" if it wasn't broken, because it certainly felt like it was.

I injured this same foot a few years later in the mine when I jumped from the rail car our crew was riding, to throw the track switch for leaving a sidetrack but before I could throw the switch the operator of the rail vehicle "ran the switch," causing the switch handle to flip up and slam down on top of my foot that I had injured in the rock fall incident. Again, I had to take a few days off and was out a new pair of boots when the boot had to be cut off my foot to examine it. The X-ray revealed no break but that was the second time the breaking of my foot had missed a good chance.

On one occasion I was a witness to an unfortunate accident that my friend and neighbor Bill Blair suffered while working as a miner helper on one section I worked on in the #1 mine. This particular section had coal of nearly seven feet in height and 18 to 24 inches of drawrock over the coal. I had dumped a load of coal into the feeder and went back for another load of coal and backed into a break while waiting for the other shuttle car to get loaded so I could pull under the miner. I could see Bill as he was standing near the miner while handling the miner cable, keeping it away from the miner's cats (tracks). I was watching the whole scene as the rib and drawrock suddenly gave way and fell on Bill, knocking him over.

From my position about 75 feet away from him, I thought he was a goner, but as I jumped from my car and rushed to him I saw his cap light shining towards the roof of the mine. Reaching him, I saw that the large rib roll had pinned one of his legs underneath it. The other shuttle car driver, the miner man, and I managed to move the rock and coal off his leg but it was obvious that his leg was broken.

One of the crew rushed to the power center and retrieved a temporary plastic arm or leg cast that was used to encase and stabilize his leg, then we got him on a stretcher and carried him to the mantrip for transport outside, then by ambulance to a hospital. The rib that had fallen on him was about 3 feet in width and about 8-9 feet high. Although the rib had caused much pain and suffering for Bill, it could easily have been much worse if the rock and coal had pinned Bill's whole body under it.

Bill was very tough and came back to work after a couple of months and resumed his miner helping job as if his leg was good as new. He had proved his toughness as a paratrooper in World War II when he was in the Army's glider troops and was one of the soldiers tasked with the occupation of Japan shortly after the end of the war.

When he worked with us he was of the age when most men were already retired but he enjoyed working as a coal miner. He had started in the mines as a teenager before going into the military. He mentioned to me that he had worked in the same mine with my grandfather, G.C. Sexton, and was working with him on the day my grandfather was fatally injured in the mine in Thornton, Kentucky.

My grandfather was injured while trying to chock the wheel of a loaded coal car, the car jumped the track and pinned him against the rib of the mine, crushing him. He lived only a few minutes after he was transported outside the mine. The date was December, 1940. That date was over 40 years before I worked with Bill at Scotia and happened years before I was born.

One interesting incident concerning rock falling from the roof of the mine happened to me when I worked on a production section after the bottom mine reopened. I worked with another miner named Roger Sturgill on the section, who was a good worker and good friend of mine who was soft-spoken and a helpful co-worker (except in this particular incident). I climbed out of the deck of my shuttle car one afternoon to move some miner cable out of the roadway and Roger, being as helpful as he usually was, moved beside me to help lift the cable and throw the loop of cable to the side.

As were standing there preparing to lift the cable, Roger looked at me and said, *"Eddie, do you owe very much?"* I looked at him with a puzzled look and wondered to myself why in the world he would pick such a time as this to ask such a question. *"What did you say Roger?"* I thought I might have misunderstood him at first. Then he repeated his words, *"Do you owe very much?"* I said, *No, I try to pay my bills as I go but I"*……. I then felt a heavy slab of drawrock hit me on top of my hard hat, nearly knocking me down. When I regained my senses and ran a few feet from the still flaking drawrock, I managed to blurt out, *"Roger! Why didn't you tell me there was loose rock over my head? If that rock had been any bigger it could have killed me!"* He looked at me with a grin on his face and said, *"Well I tried to warn you, I asked if you owed very much, you should've answered quicker!"*

After I thought about it I saw the humor in it too and Roger and I had a good laugh about it. I've often wondered what would have happened if the drawrock had been bigger than Roger thought it was. If Roger should read these words, he'll remember that incident for sure. Roger and his brother Kenneth were great to work with and I miss those days when we worked together 1,400 feet beneath Black Mountain.

One close call happened when I was working as a shuttle car operator. I bent over and picked up the miner cable to throw it out of the roadway. Just as I bent down and grasped the heavy loop of cable, a kettle bottom about the size of a five gallon bucket fell from between the roof bolts and within a few inches of my head and shoulder as it fell. If I had moved just those few inches to the left while picking up the cable I probably would have been killed or badly injured for sure. Coal mining is not for the weakhearted or easily spooked. Every miner has many close calls throughout his or her mining career. It's an invariable expectation when one works underground for any length of time.

CHAPTER TWENTY NINE

In an effort to boost the production of coal in order to hold down costs and fulfill their coal orders, Scotia introduced longwall mining in the #1 mine in 1986. This method of mining had been in use in the U.S. since the 1960's but had never yet been tried in any Blue Diamond mine. Longwall mining is similar to pillowing using conventional methods but is done on a bigger scale and with different equipment, and is much more productive than conventional mining.

The equipment used is also much more complicated to use and set up to begin producing and takes several weeks to move the equipment into place. The three main pieces are the roof jacks which are as large as an average sized automobile, a rotating cutter head, and the beltline. As the rotating head, similar to a continuous miner head, cuts the coal from the pillar of coal, the coal falls onto the belt and the coal travels on the belt to the tailgate entry where it dumps onto another belt leading to the outside of the mine.

The beltline is 48in. wide and a tremendous amount of coal is carried outside during a shift of coal production. When the cutting heads reaches the end of a block, (between 200-1,000 foot long,) the cutting head moved up a few feet in the void left from the coal cut, and the safety jacks are moved up also, allowing the rock behind the jacks to fall in, which relieves some pressure on the roof of the mine.

A study was made in the 1980's by the U.S. Department of the Interior, Bureau of Mines, in the Scotia mine, with Blue Diamond's permission and cooperation which found that:

Topography in the area is extremely mountainous, and the depth of cover over the mine ranges from near 0 to 2,000 feet. The seam being mined is the Imboden, which is typically 6 to 7 feet thick.

The immediate roof in the mine is predominantly sandstone and is generally quite stable during development. The sandstone can be massive, but it is more often crossbedded and interbetted with shale, silty shale, and some coal spars. In most areas the sandstone is underlain by 0 to 8 feet of weak shale locally known as drawrock. The drawrock is highly slickensided and of poor geotechnical quality. Where the drawrock is thin, it presents few stability problems and is often removed during mining. Where the drawrock is thicker, it tends to separate from the overlying sandstone, resulting in roof falls. Several locations (within the Scotia mine) were observed in which 20 ft. spans of thick-shale drawrock had collapsed within hours after they were mined. Few falls of the sandstone roof occurred, but in one instance an intersection with a large effective span collapsed 6 months after it had been mined.

The overburden above the immediate roof consists of more than 70 percent sandstone, including a number of massive beds. The mine floor is predominantly shale, which is prone to heaving at greater depths of cover.

The first three longwall panels at Scotia were developed in an older part of the mine, under approximately 1,000 feet of cover. A conventional three-entry, yield abutment pillar design was used in the gates of these panels, with pillars on 48 and 120 foot centers.

Longwall mining was later moved to a large area of coal reserves that was located under much greater cover. A series of panels, each measuring 700 feet wide by 7,000 feet long was expected to be mined.

The longwall poured the coal out but required thousands of timbers to be used in timbering during the mining process. The timbering was not the typical one timber at a time being installed from the mine roof to the floor of the mine, but was instead the building of crib works to support the roof. The cribs were on four foot centers and the timbers were 8in, square and in length varied from 4 ft. to 6 ft. depending on the height and condition of the roof. Some cribs were over 10ft. high and had to be scaled and built one crib block at a time. My last timbering that I did before the mine closed was in an area where the cribs were about 12 crib blocks in height and my brother Jimmy and I were the only ones doing the cribbing. We had a miserable night trying to catch up on the cribbing, especially since Jimmy was just back from a spinal disc operation and still was expected to build cribs like a well man, but he managed to make the shift, although in pain throughout the night. He might say he had a memorable shift of work.

When a longwall section finished a pillar and began the move to another area of the mine, all hands had to be on deck. Each piece of equipment (and there were several dozen of heavy safety jacks, weighing tons by themselves), had to be moved to the new area one piece at a time by rail locomotives. As my last days were spent on the track crew, first on the midnight shift, then on the day shift, we were always involved with helping with the move to the new area. Any "extra" time we had we spent on the crib building and longwall moves. That is, any extra time when we weren't laying steel rails, shoveling the belts, rock dusting the mine, working on the sections as a shuttle car driver, bolt machine operator, scoop operator, utility man, or building cribs which was a job where you were never, ever, caught up.

After Arch Mineral of St. Louis Missouri, acquired Scotia Coal from the Blue Diamond Coal Company in the fall of 1990, some improvements, modifications, and adjustments were made to Scotia's longwall system. A new style shield (or safety Jack) carrier was used, allowing shields to be moved more quickly, making for easier, more efficient set ups. Also several safety features were added to the shields during the move from the #9 panel of the Scotia mine, to the #10 panel of the mine. Hoses and controls were repositioned to eliminate tripping hazards and pinch points to allow for safer operator positioning, among other safety improvements.

A great deal of work also went into the belt system that was expected to further enhance productivity of the longwall system. Over 9,000 feet of beltline was changed out, and a belt drive was eliminated. With the change, Cumberland River Coal, (the name was changed from Scotia Coal to Cumberland River Coal when Arch Mineral Corporation bought Scotia in 1990) had 13 belts leading to the coal stockpile instead of the original 16. The new conveyor system then employed had a higher grade belt, and had a controlled start transmission as opposed to solid state starters.

In early 1991, the panel they were mining was plagued with problems. Geologic conditions severely limited production, and a roof fall prevented the extraction of equipment from the tailgate area. The roof was so poor in many areas that a new type of support was devised. The new type of support involved a heavy wire mesh that was installed in front of every fourth shield by bolting the mesh to the mine roof.

After the improvements were made to the longwall, Coordinator Thurman Holcomb pointed out that every effort had been made to improve equipment and conditions. *"Now it's up to us to prove that we CAN produce* (coal). *We need dedication and commitment, and we must realize that production means job security,"* he said. *"We must keep our minds on our jobs and really maximize our efficiency."*[23]

When Arch Mineral Corporation of St. Louis Missouri acquired the Scotia properties from Blue Diamond Coal Company in September, 1990, they renamed Scotia Coal Company, Cumberland River Coal Company. Another Arch Company, the Kyva Coal Company, con-

---

[23] Kyva News, August, 1991.

trolled several of Arch's coal companies, including their newly acquired and renamed Cumberland River Coal Company. All these name changes were pretty confusing, even for those of us who worked there at the time of the name changes.

By May of 1991, Kyva Coal had invested over $13 million dollars at the Cumberland River Coal Company. The President of Kyva Coal at the time, (Gerald Peacock), had high hopes and goals for Cumberland River Coal, one of which involved safety. In an interview in a Kyva publication called "_Kyva News_, May, 1991, President Peacock had this to say about some of his concerns concerning their new acquisition, Cumberland River Coal:

Question: What are your goals for Kyva Coal, and how will you reach them?

Mr. Peacock: Our number one goal at Kyva is to be the safest, most productive miners in the world. Safety and productivity go hand-in hand and I insist that each employee make safety his/her top priority.

Safety is a major concern at Kyva and we are working to correct the wrongs of the past. In the first six months of 1990, the Scotia property, (formerly Blue Diamond), received more MSHA violations than all of

Arch Mineral Corporation subsidiaries combined over the previous TWO years. We cannot tolerate that type of performance, and we have taken drastic measures to correct these problems. We've initiated several programs to help us improve our safety performance and if each employee commits himself to these programs, they will be effective.

In the early stages of the Arch acquisition, (of Scotia), we actually shut down production several times until a possible safety problem was corrected. This is the kind of commitment that we have to safety. Being the "safest, most productive miners in the world," is not a wish...it is a goal. And we WILL achieve it. First, we want a safe property—then a profitable one. Once we have these two factors in place, we will have job security.

Question: What are your first impressions of KYVA Coal?

Mr. Peacock: I believe that KYVA has an excellent resource that will prove to be the most valuable in its future success... the human resource. The people of all the mines (at Scotia) are willing and eager to make changes. I am very impressed with their hunger for knowledge and adaptability. They have proven to be a reliable workforce with a "can-do" attitude.

I could easily look around KYVA properties and tell you that my first impressions were not so great because I saw a monumental task of cleaning up and rebuilding. However, I will also tell you that none of the problems that we encounter will seem insurmountable in the face of our committed, dependable employees.

In his comments, one can see the President of KYVA Coal had some positive goals for Cumberland River Coal and some praise for the workforce there, but the weak coal markets and high costs associated with the mining of coal under Black mountain proved to be too difficult to overcome, as later events would prove.

In the same issue of <u>KYVA News</u>, Cumberland River Mine Manager Dan Stickel wrote this article with the headline:

Surviving the "Soft Market"

Looking around the coal industry, it is obvious that we are in one of the worst slumps our business has ever experienced. Many producers are being forced out of business, and others are being forced to streamline due to the depressed market. Reports indicate that there is over 60 million tons of surplus coal on the market. A very mild winter caused steam coal consumption to plummet and a world recession has also caused metallurgical coal consumption to drop considerably in recent months.

The law of supply and demand has forced both steam and met coal prices down so low that many producers are being forced out of business. Many of our (coal producing) neighbors have already cut back, shut down, or sold out.

We at CRCC are fortunate to be given a chance to turn our operation into a safe, productive and profitable one. We have been given the financial support that most coal operations only dream about. It is our obligation to see that we do not fail our owners. We owe them a return on their investment.

In the six months since the acquisition of CRCC we have spent $13 million to improve safety and productivity. We have lost money every month except one, (February, 1991) since the acquisition. Even with our poor performance to date and the depressed market, we have been given the financial backing to turn things around, but now our grace period is almost over. We are almost ready to move into our first Collier's Creek longwall panel... and it's time to produce in a

safe, cost-effective manner. Failure to do so will ulti-
mately jeopardize the future of CRCC and our own job
security.

CRCC reserves are some of the best quality coal
in the world. We have a market advantage in most cas-
es because of our high quality. This advantage is mean-
ingless if our cost is too high to make a profit. We have
no sales contracts at CRCC, so all our coal is sold on the
spot market. The spot market is fiercely competitive due
to the surplus of coal. Only the lowest cost spot produc-
ers will be able to sell their coal.

CRCC is budgeted to produce over 2 million tons
of coal in 1991. Marketing only has commitments for
931,000 tons. Unless our costs are reduced, we cannot
expect to sell any additional coal. We must face the
challenge of reducing our costs or suffer the conse-
quences.

We must not become discouraged. With our qual-
ity advantage we can expect to market our coal if our
cost is competitive. The best way to reduce our cost is by
improving our productivity. Tons per man shift is the
key. Our cost drops quickly when our tons per man shift
figure improves. We need to DOUBLE the current figure
of 15 tons per man shift if we are to be competitive. With
all of the recent improvements, changes in procedures

and financial support, we should be able to reach and even surpass our goals. We have the tools, we have the skills, now let's do it.

Mine management was obviously positive about the future of the CRCC in the early months of 1991, but in the end, slow sales erased the positivity and replaced it with negativity. Only four months after the above comments were expressed in the *KYVA News* publication of May, 1991, the workers at the old Scotia mines were informed of the mine closure of the Cumberland River Coal Company. Our benefits would end on December 12, 1991.

Mine manager Dan Stickel commented thus in the letter informing the workers of the closure:

Finally, we regret that we are forced to take this action. As you know, Cumberland River Coal Company is attempting to develop and mine additional reserves. To date, these efforts have not been successful. We remain committed to mine our property. At the earliest, this will not happen until next year. We hope you will continue to support us in our efforts.

Sincerely

Dan Stickel

Mine Manager

The closing of the old Scotia mine ended my coal mining career forever. A lot of former Scotia miners were later recalled when the company moved their operations to Virginia and many retired from there as the years passed. I was recalled to work there also but after traveling to the mine in Virginia and testing to make sure I could operate at least three pieces of mining equipment, (that was the requirement for all recalled miners), I decided to keep the job and new career I had started when the mine closed. I retired in 2005 after 42 years of labor, with more than 17 of those working years being spent in the bowels of the coal mines of Big Black Mountain. The memories of those days, including the good, the bad, the ugly, and the sad, will forever remain a part of me.

CHAPTER THIRTY

MORE SCOTIA MEMORIES

In 1977 I attended mine foreman certification school at the vocational school located in Whitesburg, Kentucky and received my Assistant Mine Foreman certification papers. I didn't have enough time as a coal miner to qualify for a First Class Mine Foreman certification but could still act as a foreman on a section when needed.

The test and school was the same for either certification, but time and experience was the criteria for First Class papers. In 1980 I received my Mine Foreman certification First Class papers and acted as a section foreman on occasion but turned down an offer for a permanent job, preferring to retain my seniority and time as a Scotia Employees Association member.

I liked the people I worked with and wanted to finish my mining career without the stress of being in management and having to pressure my friends for "more production, more production." Of course not all managers and foremen were of the ilk to cause stress and misery among the workers and those that bossed with a grain of compassion tended to be the ones with the highest production sections.

I had a lot of great bosses during my mining days at Scotia and I will always appreciate their civility and friendship through the years. I have already named a few that I worked with, and for, while at Scotia, and there were many others through the years that impressed me as great people.

Jerry Gilliam was a Safety Department worker that gave the workers, including me, some of our safety classes, and who later became the section boss where I was a shuttle car driver. He knew we were experienced miners on that section and he never raised his voice and gave us leeway to do our jobs. He knew how to boss and we thought a lot of him on my section. He later became the Outside Foreman for the Cumberland River Coal Company.

Another good boss that had the respect of the men was Eddie Taylor, who also knew how to supervise a section of miners and always got the best out of the crew, while doing it with thoughtfulness and with putting undue stress on the crew. He later became a Federal Mine Inspector.

Other section and mine foremen I knew and respected through the years I will mention here, while asking the forgiveness of any that I might have forgotten because of the passage of time; Bruce Jones, Wayne McDougall, Merle Rhodes, Ben Rose, Don Williams, John Fuller, Carl Petrey, David McKnight, Harvey Creech, Hargus Maggard (Electrician), and track boss Jerry McCowan.

The coal miners I worked with that were Scotia Employees Union members are too numerous to mention, encompassing nearly 400 or 500 men and women over the years at Scotia. I'm sure there are many good friends and casual acquaintances I knew while working there that I have forgotten with the passage of time, but they were all good people. They just wanted to work and provide for their families while doing the best job they could at the same time. Several of those good and decent men and women were characters, you might say. A few of their stories and actions are worth telling here.

Dan was a good repairman and a former Marine Corps veteran. He and I enjoyed reminiscing about boot camp and the many events we had experienced incidental to our training at Parris Island. He was a very tall man and had some trouble getting around the low mine height we were working in at the time. He kept the men on section laughing with his cockamamie yarns of the experiences in life he had been a part of.

One day he came to work in a brand new Chevrolet pickup truck he had just bought. We sat in the bathhouse before work time listening to his comical story of how he talked the salesman down to a super (he said) price on the truck.

After his telling of a few comical stories he rose to leave the bathhouse as work time neared. As he was leaving I said, *"Dan, wait a minute and I'll go with you and check out your new ride." I ain't got time Eddie,"* he said. *"Why not, Dan?" "I've got to go by the tipple and get a load of coal."* At that time Scotia had a small loading point where Scotia miners could get a load of house coal from them. I thought he was joking about the coal, but as I headed to my car in the parking lot I saw his brand spanking new truck parked under the tipple coal chute and the blocks of coal falling into his truck bed, with the paint job of his bed and fenders being bombarded with coal and the coal dust swirling.

I couldn't believe my eyes as I watched those big blocks of house coal falling into his truck bed. He actually wasn't joking about getting a load of coal in his "just off the showroom" new truck.

When he arrived at New Taggart with his load of coal and came into the light house where I was putting my cap light on my mining hat, I asked him, *"Dan, why in the world would you put a load of coal into your new truck and let it be beat to death like that.*" He grinned and replied, "*Buddy, I bought that truck to haul things in, and by golly, I'm gonna haul stuff in it!*" I couldn't argue with his logic but could never understand how someone could damage a paint job in a brand new vehicle that he had driven out of the showroom at Hazard, Kentucky that very morning. That was my friend Dan though, with his "never a care in the world" attitude.

Coal miners like to have fun while they're working, which serves to release some tension and interrupt the drudgery that's nearly always   present when danger lurks around every corner of the mine. Once a Scotia miner snuck around the power center and proceeded to tie a nearly impossible to loosen, knot in one of his co-worker's coat sleeves. He had one knot tied and was in the process of tying the other when the owner of the coat walked up and seeing what was happening, hollered, "*Hey! What in the h.... are you doing by tying a knot in* my *jacket?*" The knot tier thought fast and as he threw the jacket towards its owner, said "Here! *Tie it your d... self if you don't like the way I'm tying it!*" That relieved the tension and a good laugh was had by all concerned.

Another incident occurred when a co-worker was chasing miners with a rubber black snake as they were changing clothes and taking showers. Our light house man was deadly afraid of snakes, even rubber ones, so the jokester knew he could scare at least one person that would be in the bathhouse area when he brought his snake in. I was busy changing clothes when he reached the snake's head to me and I said, *"Here, let me hold that snake, I'm not afraid of it!"* After seeing I wasn't scared of his rubber snake, he said, *"No, let me scare the light-house man and listen to him holler!"* I watched as he went up to the man and held out the snake, which prompted the lighthouse worker to let out a howl and take off through the building, squalling to the top of his voice as he ran from the rubber snake.

In a few minutes the snake man came back past my wire clothes hanger and I looked and noticed the snake's tongue darting back and forth from its mouth. At that precise moment it hit me that the snake wasn't a rubber snake, but a REAL snake. To say that my legs went weak would be an understatement. I only reached for it earlier because I thought no sane person would have brought a real snake into a bathhouse full of men, but I was wrong.

I was glad that the snake holder thought I wasn't afraid of snakes and moved on when I first asked to hold it. I would have likely had a heart attack if he had handed it to me.

The Scotia coal miners always enjoyed a good trick or joke and most of them never seemed to hold a grudge even when the joke might occasionally be carried too far. I know of one instance where a miner hid a fellow miner's work car in a snow bank at night and that night even more snow fell, completely covering the car. The owner didn't find his ride until the snow melted a week or so later. Until he located his car he had to hitch a ride to Upper Taggart every evening. He never found out who the culprit was and the guilty party never publicly confessed his deed. It was all in fun and no harm was done, except for the ego.

CHAPTER THIRTY ONE

I n the late 80's the Self Contained Self Rescu-er (SCSR) became available for coal miners to use. The SCSR provided one hour of com-pressed oxygen that was designed to fasten onto the min-ing belt for quick access in case of an emergency. The canister could be stored from a 14 degrees F. to a 130degree F. range.

The in-service storage life of the self-rescuer was three years, or when used, whichever comes first. After use or three years of service, the unit had to be refur-bished and tested by a certified person before it was dis-tributed for use again.

The SCSR we were issued was made by the CSE Corporation of Monroeville, Pennsylvania. The metal container that enclosed the one hour oxygen cylinder held the 15 parts that made up the SCSR:

1. Oxygen Cylinder
2. Oxygen Cylinder Valve
3. Oxygen Pressure Gauge
4. Pressure Reducing Valve
5. Demand Valve
6. Oxygen Hose
7. Breathing Bag

8. Carbon Dioxide Absorber

9. Heat Exchanger

10. Breathing Hose

11. Mouth Piece

12. Nose Clamp

13. Relief Valve

14. Relief Valve Chamber

15. By-Pass Hose

Every SCSR had a pressure gauge that had to be checked when using or checking and the needle had to be in the green or yellow before using. The instructions for using are as follows in seven steps.

1. Read pressure

2. Open valve

3. Place around neck

4. Pull mouthpiece plug

5. Insert mouthpiece

6. Nose clamp

7. Goggles

When these life-saving devices were first introduced to Scotia miners in the late 80's we had extensive training in using them. Every Scotia miner had to practice opening and putting the canister's apparatus on, including the mouthpiece. We were taught the seven steps necessary to use the device. With the disasters of the past still fresh in everyone's mind, we watched and listened attentively when the safety instructor was demonstrating their use. None of us wanted to have a repeat of having several men die because of the lack of oxygen. One hour's oxygen would have likely have saved the lives of the six men who had barricaded in the heading of 2 Left Panel after the first explosion.

When the new SCSR devices were first introduced I was a shuttle car operator in the bottom mine. We usually kept the canisters stored in the power center, which was the central meeting place for all the section men. We held safety meetings there, our mine phone communications were located there, and we always ate our dinner there because of the warmth the power center generated. Most of the time miners sat on top of the 7,200 volt box where they could warm up while eating.

After the first canisters were introduced, we soon were issued a smaller version of the canister which also carried a one hour supply of oxygen. These were smaller than the original canisters and it was possible to wear one while operating a piece of equipment, but it was very tight in the cramped deck of the shuttle car and sometimes your SCSR became tangled with the controls of the car, causing the operator to lose time while straightening the mess out. The problem was somewhat solved by obtaining permission from the boss to tale our canisters off our belts and storing them under our car seats. The regulations stated that we had to be within 50 feet of our oxygen canisters at all times.

When we had to help the continuous miner set up in a different entry we sometimes had to exceed the regulation limit concerning keeping within the 50 ft. distance. There was no other solution for it because we had to ready to act to help keep the continuous miner from running over heavy cable loops which had to be thrown out of the path of the miner's tracks.

On one occasion, my fellow shuttle car operator, Ellis Hill, was wondering over the section somewhere when an MSHA Inspector happened upon the section to conduct an inspection. Observing Ellis running around the section without his oxygen container, at least 200-300 feet from his canister, which was stored under his shuttle car seat, the inspector stopped Ellis to question him. Inspector: *"Ellis, where's your oxygen canister?"* Ellis replied, *"It's under my shuttle car seat!"* *"Now Ellis, you know you're supposed to be wearing it!"* Ellis looked the inspector in the eye and said in a loud voice,

"Buddy I'm allowed 50 feet!" The inspector just shook his head, turned around, and walked away with a grin of his own.

Ellis was always quite a jokester while working around a group of men and the inspector knew Ellis and nearly all of us by name so he enjoyed the moment along with Ellis and me. Ellis did take the hint though and retrieved his canister from his shuttle car which he wore until the inspector left the section.

Once when we were working to reach the bodies of the eleven men who were killed in the second explosion, a group of Federal Inspectors were climbing aboard the few buses available that were parked at the bottom of the slope. They were all trying to scrouge into the few seats available, even doubling up on the two locomotives waiting there, with six or more in each bus compartment.

Elis watched as the inspectors, all of them higher ups from Pennsylvania and even Washington, D.C., finally settled down for the trip with their reflective clothing and snooty attitudes of, 'I'm here and in control and all is well.' Ellis then thought it was time for his act.

"What do you all think you are doing," he shouted over all the chatter going on. *"You're overcrowding the mantrips, you know better than that!"* Now act like

you know what you're doing and get outta them man-trips and off them motors!"

When he said that to all the brass I thought that he'd catch it for sure from so many officials he had just chastised and embarrassed. You could have heard a pin drop by the silence after his tirade, but instead, the Federal people sheepishly unpacked themselves from the mantrips and proceeded to select just a few to go on the available transportation. Ellis stood there like he was someone in authority while his co-workers were trying hard not to laugh out loud, knowing to ourselves that Ellis was putting on an act, having no more authority than any shuttle car operator who might pass by the group.

Our crew then walked to our mantrip , which had been parked in front of all the others. We piled into our mantrip and proceeded down the track towards our fresh air base to build seals. As we went along Ellis was listening to all our comments about how he "sure put those Federal Inspectors in their place," while he lay back in the bus grinning like crazy. We ribbed him constantly afterwards about putting the brass out of the mantrips that day.

Ellis was normally the quietest man on the section and wouldn't harm a fly but he gave us all a good laugh after the brass thought he must be a high Company or

Federal official when he scolded them that day. We all though the world of Ellis and his antics.

When Cumberland River closed down their Scotia mine on December 12, 1991, they laid off 293 hourly workers and about 100 salaried employees, while leaving 18 hourly workers to close up the mine. The total count was 411 miners who were losing their jobs, at least temporarily. Some, including me would never return to mining, while many others would eventually be called back and woke several years afterward for Cumberland River Coal Company, in other locations.

When the layoff of Scotia's workforce took place, the company's general counsel stated that the company would help laid-off workers find new jobs. The only problem with that was that hardly any coal mining jobs were available anywhere during that period of time.

Most Scotia employees had been working for Scotia for ten years or more and many were in their 40's and fifties, (some even in their 50's and 60's) and even if jobs had been available, what company would want to hire a miner who was near retirement age? The pickings were slim and few miners found other jobs immediately after the layoff.

I know that I put in several applications in and around Letcher and Knott County but never received even an inquiry from prospective employers. The coal slowdown of that period had been a big factor in the closing of Cumberland River Coal and the timing of the mine closure could not have been worse.

Scotia miners who were from Letcher County were directed to attend a job assessment and testing class hosted by the Kentucky State Unemployment division at the Vocational School in Ermine, Kentucky. After the testing, which included the testing the educational grade level and mechanical ability of each laid off miner, nothing more came of the results as far as obtaining employment.

We were basically on our own, and that's how we eventually secured employment again, by our own efforts. Eventually most, if not all of the Scotia miners found other jobs, in a few mines and other industries, and a few miners retired.

I appreciated my job at Scotia and don't regret my 6,216 days as a Scotia coal miner, but I do regret the loss of so many friends and co-workers that lost their lives beneath Black Mountain. May we always remember and never forget the sacrifice they made while working to support their families.

APPENDIX

Cumberland River Coal Company
HC 67, Box 1290
Cumberland, Kentucky 40823
606-633-4422   Fax: 606-633-1277

NOTICE

TO: All Employees

FROM: Dan Stickel

DATE: May 9, 1991

SUBJECT: Realignment of CRCC Employees to Five (5) day work week.

Effective May 11, 1991 the following work schedules will be implemented at Cumberland River Coal Company. Please check the posted work schedule for your assigned shift and crew. If you have a question concerning your assigned shift or crew you must inform your supervisor no later than May 15, 1991.

The change in our work schedule was necessary for Cumberland River Coal Company to be competitive within a very slumping coal market. Working together to make changes happen continue to promote our reputation as being a reliable and dependable mining operation.

Respectfully,

Dan Stickel

Dan Stickel

Cumberland River Coal Co. Roster, 1991,
Courtesy of Mike Halcomb

326

BLACK MOUNTAIN ELEGY

SHOP

	1ST SHIFT (8 - 4)	2ND SHIFT (4 - 12)	3RD SHIFT (12 - 8)
Elect.	Bill Bedwell	T. Kincer(OI)	
1st Cl. Repair	Bobby Collins David Smith Mike Dingus	Bobby Baker(OI)	
Truck Driver	Adean Adams	Wm. P. Hatfield	Harvey Coker
Extra Man	Bill Maggard(OI)		

327

BLACK MOUNTAIN ELEGY

PREPARATION PLANT

(Monday thru Friday Crew)

	1st Shift (8 - 4)	2nd Shift (4 - 12)	3rd Shift (12 - 8)
Pl. Oper.	Harold Cornett B. F. Caudill	Clark Surber Charles Shepherd	
Coal Flow	Sam Sparkman Wayne Cornett	Harrison Stidham Denver Gross	
X-Oper.	Tommy Gross	Frank Collins	
HEO	Paul Maggard Sr. David J. Craiger	Roy Perry David Fields	Carl Bowling
Repair	Ernest Collins	James Cornett	Gary Campell Jonah Branham James Caudill Roy Huff Mefferd Holbrook Ben Bentley Eddie Bentley
Greaser	Jerry Huff		Wayne Wilson
Cleanup	Ellis Hill		Mike Duff Claude Shepherd
Mechanic	Willie Perry		

NOTE: These are the tentative Schedules for 5 day work week, to begin May 11, 1991 (Saturday). If you feel you are placed wrongly, see or get word to Eddie Durbin.

328

BLACK MOUNTAIN ELEGY

<u>PREPARATION PLANT</u>

(Thursday thru Monday Crew)

<u>1st Shift</u> (8 - 4)	<u>2nd-Shift</u> (4 - 12)	<u>3rd Shift</u> (12 - 8)
HEO	Daniel G. Bentley		
Elect.	Danny Polli		
Repair	Van Webb Lonnie D. Ison William Varner Paul H. Maggard Jr. David Webb Jr. Dennis Combs Rex Conley	Charles Pease	

NOTE: These are the tentative Schedules for 5 day work week, to begin May 11, 1991 (Saturday. If you feel you are placed wrongly, see or get word to Eddie Durbin.

BLACK MOUNTAIN ELEGY

ODD CREW

SATURDAY THRU WEDNESDAY

3rd Shift (1:30 A.M. - 9:30 A.M.)

1st Class Longwall Repairman	Henry Lewis
1st Class Repairman	Wilburn Shepherd
1st Class Repairman	Wendell Bates
1st Class Repairman	Mark Penley
GI	Billy J. Adams
GI	Tim Cantrell
GI	Hosea Dunson
GI	James F. Morris
GI	Tim Vanover
GI	Roger Teague
GI	Greg Boggs
GI	Jerry Bush
GI	Herman J. Fields
GI	Jeff Couch
GI	Jeff Begley
GI	Johnny Warren
GI	Roger Cornett
Section Utility	Myrel Lewis
Section Utility	Ricky Sparks
Section Utility	William D. Hatfield
GI	Bobby Stamper
GI	Jackie Littrell
Shearer Operator	Ben Kincer
Shield Operator	Mike Wells
Shield Operator	Tim Wright
Headgate Operator	Bill Rose

330

ODD CREW

4TH SHIFT

Wednesday thru Sunday (7:00 P.M. - 3:00 A.M.)

1st Class Longwall Repair	Danny Adams
1st Class Longwall Repair	Malla Addington
1st Class Longwall Repair	Eddie Davidson (OI)
1st Class Longwall Repair	Dale Dickerson (OI)
1st Class Repair	David Cornett
1st Class Repair	Greg Mayhew
1st Class Repair	Doyle Fields
1st Class Repair	Michael Ison
1st Class Repair	Carlos Combs
1st Class Repair	George Widner
1st Class Repair	James Craft
1st Class Repair	Rick Campbell
Belt Repairman	Jerry Johnson
Sectional Utility	Roger Burke
GI/Scoop	Floyd Thompson
Beltman	Tom Brigmon
Beltman	Luther Halcomb
Beltman	Meshak Holcomb
Beltman	Paul Lark
Beltman	Billy Banks
GI	Sonny Adams
Shield Operator	Rory Blair
GI	Albert Smith
GI	David A. Sturgill
Headgate Oper.	Walker Bentley
GI	Gary Caldwell
GI	Cullen Shepherd
GI	Mike Hatfield
GI	Elizabeth Rigney
GI	Roger Smith
GI	Bobby Maggard Jr.
GI	Ricky Hatfield
GI	Winfrey Bowman
GI	Benny Hart
GI	
GI	
Motorman	Denvil Gibson
Motorman	Ronald Halcomb
Lamphouse Man	Lawrence Stephens
2nd Class Repair	Larry Nease
Shield Operator	Don Walker
Shearer Operator	Herman L. K. Smith

BLACK MOUNTAIN ELEGY

```
                    UNDERGROUND CREWS

                    Monday thru Friday

                        1ST SHIFT

                  (8:00 A.M. - 4:00 P.M.)


                    1 Rt.                    2 Rt.

Cont. Miner Oper.   Benny Adams              Bobby Mullins

Roof Bolter         Donnie Cornett           James McKnight
Roof Bolter         James Spangler           Jerry Kirk

Car Driver          Larry Brock              Harold Lewis
Car Driver          Wm. Sconce               Wm. Collier

Miner Helper        Johnny Fields            Jesse Craft

Sectional Utility   Donald Dixon             Enoch Maggard

G I                 David Day                Allen Branham

1st Class Repair    Lonzo Day                Alan Dicks
```

BLACK MOUNTAIN ELEGY

```
                    UNDERGROUND CREW

                    Monday thru Friday

                       2ND SHIFT

                  (2:30 P.M. - 10:30 P.M.)


                  1 Rt.                  2 Rt.

Cont. Miner Oper.  Henry Halcomb         Mack Brock

Roof Bolter        Brad Whitaker         Disney Miniard
Roof Bolter        Gary Potter           Leonard Adams

Car Driver         Harold Nelson         Doyle Perry
Car Driver         Leroy Fields          Roger Sturgill

Miner Helper       Ralph Little          Danny Hatfield

Sectional Utility  Greg Addington        Millard Smith

G.I.               James Forester        Thomas Cornett

1st Cl. Repair     Dale Lewis            Doug Johnson
```

```
                         UNDERGROUND CREW

                         Monday thru Friday

                            3RD SHIFT

                       (1:30 A.M. - 9:30 A.M.)


                         1 Rt.                    2 Rt.

Cont. Miner Oper.        Willard Boggs            Hansford Barker

Roof Bolter              Gary Sexton              Jerry McFall
Roof Bolter              Johnny Littrell          Charles Yeary

Car Driver               J. L. Boggs              Henry Day
Car Driver               Jimmy Hall               Thomas Fields

Miner Helper             Wilma Caudill            Tommy Niece

Sectional Utility        Bruce Outlaw             George Potter

G I                      Barry Fleming            Larry S. Adams

1st Cl. Repair           Wm. Tucker               Gary J. Baker
```

BLACK MOUNTAIN ELEGY

BLACK MOUNTAIN ELEGY

```
                    UNDERGROUND CREW

                    Monday thru Friday

                       LONGWALL


                1ST SHIFT        2ND SHIFT         3RD SHFIT
                (8 - 4)          (2.30 - 10:30)    (1:30AM-9:30AM)

Shearer Oper.   Ronald Sumpter   Albert Church     Jerry Bentley
Shearer Oper.   Larry Childers   Carlos Sturgill   Emmitt McElroy

Shield Oper.    Gary Joe Shelton Leonard Halcomb   Jeff Roberts
Shield Oper.    Sam Foutch       Paul Kemplin      Roy McKnight
Shield Oper.    John Hayes       Vernon Church     Danny Fields

Headgate Oper.  Darrell Smith    David Morris      Oliver Sexton
Headgate Oper.  Acley Potter     Bill Kilbourn     Roger Yeary

1st Cl. LW Rep. Dennis Wells     James Owens       Ricky Jones
1st Cl. LW Rep. James M. Pease   James Burns
```

UNDERGROUND CREW

OUTBY

Monday thru Friday

1st Shift

(8:00 A.M. - 4:00 P.M.)

1st Class Repairman	James Miles
Belt Repairman	Melbourn McKnight
Belt Repairman	James Gross
Motorman	Tone Gross
Motorman	Paul Fields
Pumpman	James Caldwell
Pumpman	Baylus Caudill
Lamphouse	Wm. Cantrell
2nd Cl. Rep.	Stephen Miles
GI	Benny Yates
GI	Ronnie Caudill
GI	Larry Cornett
GI	Larkin Napier
GI	James Cross
GI	Mike Halcomb
GI	Don Caudill
GI	Roger Bowman
GI	Ronald Warf
GI	Rickey Sturgill
GI	Lonnie Mosley
GI	James Sergent
GI	Delmas Cornett
GI	Lewis Brown
GI	Bobby Kilbourn
Beltman	Billy Bowman
Beltman	Elmer Bowman
Beltman	Jimmy Scott
Beltman	Jack Branham
Beltman	David W. Sturgill
Beltman	Eddie Gibson
Timberman	Darwin Mcknight
Timberman	Wesley Rosenbaum
Timberman	Arthur Jackson
Timberman	Danny Roberts
Timberman	Roy Sage
Telephone Repairman	Roscoe Holbrook

```
                         UNDERGROUND CREW

                             OUTBY

                       Monday thru Friday

                           2ND SHIFT

                    (2:30 P.M. thru 10:30 P.M.)
```

Motorman	Bennett Adams
Motorman	Carl Banks
Trackman	Junior Paul Fields
Trackman	Bristo Cornett
Trackman	Frank Cecil
Trackman	Jack E. Roberts
Trackman	Eddie Nickels
2nd Cl. Repair	John Perry
GI	Marion Profitt
GI	Jack Cornett
GI	Eugene Mooneyhan
GI	Randall Huff
GI	Richard Lark
GI	Hank Craft
GI	Gary Miles
GI	Jim Banks
GI	Bolivar Sexton
GI	Arthur Miles
GI	Garland Ison
GI	Jerry Dixon
GI	Steve Brock
Belt Repairman	Kenneth Sturgill
Belt Repairman	Bobby Maggard Sr.
Beltman	John Galloway
Beltman	John Caudill
Beltman	Daniel Maggard
Beltman	Paul L. Maggard
Beltman	Johnny Maggard
Beltman	Elbert Bush
Telephone Repairman	Stanley Sokolowski

BLACK MOUNTAIN ELEGY

UNDERGROUND CREW

OUTBY

Monday thru Friday

3rd Shift

(1:30 A.M. - 9:30 A.M.)

1st Class Repairman	Terry Wilson
1st Class Repairman	Ellis S. Sturgill
Motorman	Larry Barker
Motorman	Roy Jent
GI	William Hubbard
GI	David L. Sturgill
GI/Longwall	Paul Church
GI/Longwall	Phillip Evans
GI/Longwall	Tim Halcomb
GI	James Roberts
GI	David Trent
Beltman	Tim Maggard
Beltman	Robert Shackleford
Beltman	Gillis Halcomb
Beltman	Billy Sturgill
Beltman	David Dinsmore
Beltman	Norman Sturgill
Bratticeman	Edward Shepherd
Bratticeman	J. R. Franklin
Bratticeman	Greg Sumpter
Bratticeman	Larry Mullins
Bratticeman	Larry Combs (OI)

BLACK MOUNTAIN ELEGY

Letter of appreciation to Scotia's Superintendent concerning Scotia's Mine Rescue Team, which helped to suppress a mine fire in Pennsylvania in 1989.

COMMONWEALTH OF PENNSYLVANIA
DEPARTMENT OF ENVIRONMENTAL RESOURCES
Bureau of Deep Mine Safety
Fayette County Health Center
Room 167, 100 New Salem Road
Uniontown, PA 15401
December 12, 1989

Blue Diamond Coal Company
Superintendent
HC 67, Box 1290
Cumberland, KY 40823

Dear Mr. Superintendent,

We would like to express our sincere congratulations and heartfelt gratitude to the members of the Blue Diamond Coal Company, Scotia Mine Rescue Team for their relentless and courageous efforts during the recent Mathies Mine Fire.

Due to the fine work of your mine rescue team members, the security of nearly four hundred employees and their families, as well as the vast millions of resource dollars were preserved.

Under physically demanding and extremely hazardous conditions, your employees displayed the fibre indicative of their dedication to Mine Rescue, and the welfare of their fellow miners.

In keeping with the missions of both the Department of Environmental Resources, and the Bureau of Deep Mine Safety, Mr. Superintendent, I can assure you that the preservation of natural resources, and the health and safety of the Commonwealth's citizenry can only be achieved through a team effort, such as displayed at the Mathies Mine.

While it is our earnest desire to eliminate mine emergencies throughout the Commonwealth, it is reassuring to know that at the time of crisis, we can count on your employees.

Sincerely,

Thomas J. Ward, Jr.
Director
Bureau of Deep Mine Safety

BIBLIOGRAPHY

Books:

Caudill, Harry M., *Night comes to the Cumberlands*, Little, Brown, and Co., 1963

Clark-Kirkpatrick, *Exploring Kentucky*, 1960

Clark, Thomas D., *A History of Kentucky*, The John Bradford Press, Lexington, Kentucky, 1960.

Nickels, Eddie, *Scotia – Coal Mine of Doom*, Createspace 2017

Government Reports:

Mine Disasters in the United States; The United States Mine Rescue Association

Scotia Coal Mine Disaster; U. S. Government Printing Office, 1976; A Staff Report Prepared by the Staff of the House Committee on Education and Labor Standards, John H. Dent, Chairman.

Newspapers

The Chicago Tribune, Chicago, Illinois, December 8, 1978

The Courier Journal, Louisville, Kentucky, March 14, 1976

341

The Letcher County Community Press, Cromona, Kentucky, March 18, 1976

Lexington Herald-Leader; Lexington, Kentucky, November 13, 1991.

The Mountain Eagle, March through December, 1976

Periodicals:

KYVA News, Cumberland River Coal Company, May, 1991-August, 1991

United Mine Workers Journal, April, 1976

Mountain Life and Work, July, 1976

Pamphlets:

Commonwealth of Kentucky, Department of Mines and Minerals; *Surface Mining Safety Standards, Coal and Clay*, 1975

Federal Register/Vol. 73, No. 116

United States Department of the Interior; <u>Investigations to determine the cause of the explosions March 9 and 11, 1976 at the Scotia Mine in Oven Fork, Kentucky</u>, Whitesburg, Kentucky (public hearings)

United States Department of Labor, Mine Safety and
  Health Administration Review Committee; sol
  (MSHA) v. Scotia Coal 1982

Unites States Department of Labor, Mine Safety and
  health Administration; *Winter Alert Safety Manual, 1985.*

Glossary

Bore Hole – A hole drilled with a drill or rotary tool to provide access to underground sections of a mine.

Bottom – The floor in an underground mine.

Brattice – A temporary partition in an underground mine consisting of fire-resistant cloth to direct the flow of air into the working face.

Command Center – Any work area established directing response to a mine emergency.

Crosscut – A cut through a block of coal to allow access of mining equipment and the passage of air.

Curtain – A piece or sheet of fire resistant material used to direct fresh air to the working face.

Entry – A passageway about 20 ft. wide that has been mined of coal and connected to crosscuts about every 80-100 feet.

Fresh Air Base – An underground station in the intake airway established by rescue teams during rescue and recovery efforts.

Gob – Waste material produced in coal mining, such as clay, shale, etc.

Inby – In a direction toward the working face of a coal mine.

MESA – Acronym for Mine Enforcement and Safety Administration.

MHSA – Acronym for Mine Health and Safety Administration.

Motor – Another word for an underground locomotive.

Outby – In a direction toward the outside of a coal mine.

Overcast – An enclosed airway constructed to provide a means for one air current to cross another.

Panel – A compartment of a coal mine separated from other working places by a large block or several pillars of coal.

Recovery – The restoration of a whole or a part of a coal mine that has suffered damage because of roof falls, fires, explosions, water or other causes.

Regulator – An adjustable partial obstruction in an airway.

Rescue Team – A team of miners trained to work under dangerous conditions while wearing breathing apparatuses for rescue and recovery operations.

Rib – The walls or sides of a mined entry or entries in an underground coal mine.

Roof – The rock immediately above a coal seam.

Seal – The securing of an opening against the seeping or escaping of air or noxious gases from a contaminated area of the mine by building concrete barriers and sealing with mine sealant or grout.

Shaft – A vertical opening through the strata that is or may be used in connection with the mining of coal, for the purpose of ventilation or drainage, or for hoisting men, coal, or other material.

Slope – An inclined passage driven from the surface down through the strata to provide access to the mine workings.

Stopping – A wall of concrete blocks and cement or mortar used to seal or close off crosscuts to prevent air from short circuiting, so as to maintain ventilation to the working faces.

Working Face – The place where coal is extracted from the face in a heading or crosscut.

BLACK MOUNTAIN ELEGY

From Left: Steven, Alisha, Jeffrey, Wanda, Eddie

Steve: November 14, 1967 – April 11, 2018

My history loving buddy, we miss you and our hearts are saddened by our loss.

Photo courtesy of Mike Halcomb

Quilt made of old Mine Rescue Coveralls.

Index

Blackwood Land Company, **268**, **287**
Blue Diamond Coal Co, **104**, **211**
Blue Diamond Coal Company, **3**, **4**, **13**, **33**, **84**, **104**,
 145, **152**, **160**, **188**, **192**, **211**, **213**, **228**, **268**, **287**,
 302, **303**
Bob Childers, **173**
bore hole, **86**, **87**, **248**, **250**, **251**
Brad Whitaker, **202**, **216**
bratticemen, **59**
Bruce Jones, **67**, **194**, **231**, **313**
Bull Crew, **190**
Bureau of Surface Mining Inspector, **246**

 C

Carbon Monoxide, **113**
Carl Petrey, **313**
Carl Polly, **145**
carpenters, **60**
Carr's Fork, **78**
Caudill, Harry M, **341**
Cecil Davis, **103**, **105**, **118**
Charles Fields, **118**
Charles Kirk, **83**
Charles Sample, **111**, **120**
Charlie Davidson, **202**
Chevy, **12**, **27**, **34**, **74**, **77**, **78**, **80**, **81**
Clark, Thomas D., **341**
Clark-Kirkpatrick, **341**
Clemons, **120**, **140**
Clifford Smith, **289**
coal drill operator, **39**, **43**, **44**, **45**, **63**
coal dust, **23**

J

K

Kenneth Boggs, **64**
Kenneth Kiser, **135**, **145**
Kenneth Turner, **127**
Kentucky Department of Mines and Minerals, **126**, **141**
Khe Sanh, **96**
Knott, **75**
Knoxville, **33**
Koehler, **30**
Kyva Coal Company, **303**

L

Larkin Napier, **288**
Larry, **127**, **148**
Lawrence Peavey, **107**
Leatherwood, **104**, **157**
Lester Holbrook, **42**
Letcher County, **3**, **79**, **83**, **84**, **121**, **125**, **126**, **146**, **151**, **220**, **287**, **288**, **325**, **342**
lighthouse, **15**, **26**, **31**, **35**, **316**
locomotive, **16**, **17**, **18**, **20**, **62**, **70**, **71**, **84**, **90**, **100**, **101**, **107**, **124**, **132**, **143**, **196**, **198**, **209**, **218**, **223**, **225**, **238**, **272**, **345**
longwall, **298**, **300**, **301**, **302**, **303**, **307**

M

mantrip, **15**, **17**, **18**, **19**, **20**, **25**, **40**, **93**, **196**, **230**, **269**, **294**, **323**
McCreary County, Kentucky, **151**
Merle Rhodes, **313**
MESA, **3**, **82**, **97**, **102**, **103**, **110**, **111**, **126**, **128**, **129**, **132**, **134**, **135**, **136**, **138**, **139**, **141**, **142**, **148**, **156**,

Southern Labor Union, **11**, **105**
spads, **64**
Stearns, Kentucky, **268**
Steven Miles, **199**
Stickel, **306**, **309**
supplymen, **59**

T

Tallman, **202**, **203**, **204**
Tennessee, **3**, **13**, **33**, **84**, **104**, **160**, **212**, **213**, **268**
The Mountain Eagle, **73**, **157**, **160**, **220**, **227**, **342**
Thornton, **10**, **77**, **80**, **295**
Thurman Holcomb, **303**
Tim Lee Carter, **126**
Timothy Maggard, **280**, **286**
Tommy R. Scott, **127**
Tommy Gross, **202**, **238**
Torkars, **83**
trackway, **25**, **138**
trolley, **90**, **91**, **92**
Tunnel Hill, **79**

U

U.M.W.A, **247**
U.S. Steel Mine Rescue Team, **164**
United Mine Workers, **10**, **11**, **85**, **151**, **342**
Upper Taggart, **4**, **6**, **13**, **15**, **25**, **28**, **30**, **34**, **36**, **39**, **40**,
    41, **52**, **62**, **65**, **66**, **67**, **70**, **82**, **85**, **87**, **90**, **91**, **92**,
    104, **147**, **152**, **154**, **226**, **227**, **276**, **277**, **278**, **281**,
    285, **288**, **317**
Upshur, Buckhannon County, West Virginia, **245**
utility man, **28**, **37**, **43**, **58**, **63**, **64**, **288**, **302**

About the Author

Eddie Nickels is a retired Scotia coal miner and lives in Eastern Kentucky at the Western base of Pine Mountain, which is part of the Cumberland Mountains Plateau. He is the husband of one wife, the father of three, the grandfather of nine, and the great-grandfather of eight children. He is a retiree of Scotia Coal Company and in his second career he retired as a life and health insurance account representative for a large insurance and financial services company. He is a veteran of the U.S. Marine Corps, having served during the Vietnam War era.

www.ingramcontent.com/pod-product-compliance
Lightning Source LLC
LaVergne TN
LVHW051726080426
835511LV00018B/2904